THE
PROPHET'S
PULPIT

Commentaries
on the State of Islam

VOLUME I

THE PROPHET'S PULPIT

Commentaries on the State of Islam

VOLUME I

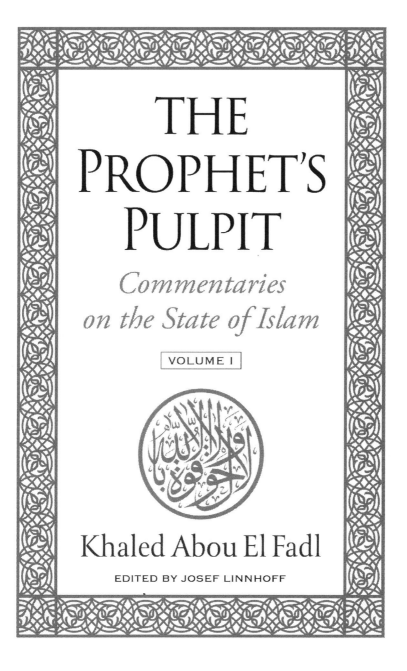

Khaled Abou El Fadl

EDITED BY JOSEF LINNHOFF

The Prophet's Pulpit: Commentaries on the State of Islam, Volume I

For information about this title or to order other books and/or electronic media, contact the publisher:

Usuli Press
715 Shawan Falls Drive, Suite 662
Dublin, OH 43017
www.usulipress.com
Email: info@usulipress.com

Usuli Press is an imprint of The Institute for Advanced Usuli Studies (The Usuli Institute).
www.usuli.org

Library of Congress Control Number (LCCN): 2022900222

ISBN's:
Hardcover Case Laminate: 978-1-957063-00-3
Hardcover Dust Jacket: 978-1-957063-04-1
Paperback: 978-1-957063-02-7
eBook: 978-1-957063-01-0
Library Bound: 978-1-957063-03-4

Printed in the United States of America

Cover design by Robin Locke Monda
Interior design by 1106 Design

The Arabic calligraphy on the front cover can be translated as "There is no strength or power except with God."

This book is dedicated to Muslims around the world suffering under injustice and oppression . . .

Contents

· · · · · · · · · · · ·

PREFACE

. . . .

I first encountered Professor Khaled Abou El Fadl's writings as a non-Muslim undergraduate student in theology. The encounter sparked an initial interest in Islamic Studies, an interest that soon grew into a passion and led to further studies, eventually culminating in a PhD degree. The same passion also led to my conversion to Islam in 2015. Yet conversion to Islam is not easy. It is much more than a change in belief or ritual; it is a major rethinking of how you see the world and everything in it. A convert enters a strange liminal space—a Muslim among friends and family, a convert among Muslims. The convert's new sense of faith is also delicate and fragile; it needs to be nurtured. In my own case, while I loved many aspects of my new-found faith, perhaps the worst thing about my new life was listening to the Friday *khutbah* (sermon). In those opening weeks and months, I remember waiting to hear to a sermon that actually addressed the real ethical issues plaguing Muslim communities. Rather than address those very real problems, most sermons were entirely divorced from reality. Most sermons were speaking a different language than the congregation—figuratively, but sometimes literally—and discussing the same select topics ad nauseam, avoiding any talk that was relevant, ethical, or thoughtful. A weekly event meant to inspire and elevate typically achieved the opposite. Was it just me? Were my expectations unrealistic? Was I attending the wrong mosque? Slowly but surely, the realization dawned: this problem was endemic. Initial enthusiasm soon gave way to confusion, bitterness, and, perhaps worst of all, apathy.

It was against this backdrop that I reconnected with the work of Professor Abou El Fadl, more specifically through the work of the then newly-established Institute for Advanced Usuli Studies ("The Usuli Institute"). I was by this time well acquainted with the Professor's writings. I knew him as a highly distinguished name in academia, widely respected as a classically trained jurist with expertise in both the Islamic and Western legal traditions. Several of his works had become classics in the field. I also knew of Professor Abou El Fadl's accomplishments in the field of human rights, including his being the first Muslim board member of *Human Rights Watch* and his receiving the University of Oslo's Human Rights Award in 2007. But what spoke to me personally through his *halaqa*s and *khutbah*s at The Usuli Institute was his honesty, candor, and awareness of the real challenges facing Muslims. The Professor spoke with a frankness that I had yet to hear in any Muslim space. His insights were rich with knowledge, experience, and, perhaps most disarmingly of all, common sense. As a jaded convert, it was exactly what I was looking for. It was like cold water to a parched soul.

I reached out to The Usuli Institute and connected with Grace Song, the Executive Director. After several conversations, Grace asked me to take the lead on collecting, editing, and publishing a collection of Professor Abou El Fadl's *khutbah*s. These *khutbah*s had already impacted me. And the more that I read, collected, and edited the volume, the more I was reminded of why I became Muslim. The work rekindled my own love for the faith.

But I was driven by something else. What if these *khutbah*s were more widely available? What if this way of thinking and talking about Islam reached a larger audience? What if more *jumu'a*s and *khutbah*s were like this? I knew that my own experiences and frustrations were not unique. I knew that so many Muslims, young and old, were looking for something more, something fresh, something to remind them of the power and beauty of their faith. So many were searching for the Islam that is expressed in this volume: an Islam of ethics, justice, and beauty; an Islam that speaks to both head and heart, rooted in the past but fully engaged with the present; an Islam that sees reason and enquiry not as enemies of faith, but as a means to faith; an Islam, quite simply, of meaning and relevance to the world. What had strengthened my own faith, I realized, could do the same for others.

There is a beautiful paradox underpinning Professor Abou El Fadl's thought. It is clearly on display in this volume. On the one hand, Professor Abou El Fadl calls for an Islam steeped in learning, knowledge, and erudition. Behind every *khutbah* stands a vast amount of reading and a mastery of the relevant discipline, whether Islamic history, theology, jurisprudence, U.S. constitutional or human rights law, among others. It is the requirement of every scholar or jurist, he states, to master the systems of knowledge of the age. Yet the current volume also calls us toward an Islam that is natural and intuitive. These *khutbah*s are not academic treatises aimed at a scholarly elite. Rather, they seek to remind *all* Muslims of some of the most basic and foundational truths of the faith. If something is unjust, ugly, or oppressive, for example, then it cannot be Islamic; Islam must above all be reasonable, make sense, and not sit heavy on the chest; Islam is more than just the performance of ritual or the minutia and mechanics of law.

It should be added to this that Professor Abou El Fadl is no armchair scholar detached from the harsh realities of life. Quite the opposite. His ideas were formed in the heat of test, trial, and suffering. There is a price to pay for Muslim scholars today who speak truth to power. Professor Abou El Fadl's stance has come at a huge personal cost. He has in the past been arrested and tortured by the Egyptian security services. He has survived several assassination attempts. To this day, he cannot enter Egypt or Saudi Arabia for fear of his personal safety. He suffers many debilitating health issues, some a direct result of these ordeals. That Professor Abou El Fadl continues to speak from the pulpit is itself a display of his intellectual courage. The act alone sets a moral example. When he calls for the imperative of justice or condemns the evils of despotism, then, these are not mere abstractions. He is speaking from personal and painful experience. Readers are encouraged to keep this background in mind.

This makes his reception in the Muslim community even more puzzling. Professor Abou El Fadl remains a voice from the margins, not the mainstream, of modern Islam. Some have accused him of being too "liberal," "progressive" or "Mu'tazili," on the one hand, or even a stealth "Islamist" and apologist for "political Islam," on the other. What is meant by these terms is often unclear. The fact that he receives criticism from all sides is perhaps best evidence of an independent intellect. But it also suggests a lack of close engagement with or understanding of his thought. In what follows, as in all his works, certain themes are so clear and consistent as to be undeniable. This includes a commitment to the Qur'an and the moral example of the Prophet Muhammad; a defense of the Islamic tradition as our anchor and guide in the present; and a love for the Muslim *Ummah*—a love sometimes expressed through harsh criticism of what the *Ummah* has become. Readers can decide for themselves what labels, if any, they find most appropriate.

I sincerely hope that the pages that follow have the same profound effect upon the reader that they had upon me. There are certain historical periods in which the test is simply to preserve a principle. The pages that follow argue clearly that the battle at present is over the very principles and ethical foundations of Islam. Does Islam mean anything to the world? Does Islam have anything to offer humanity? Is Islam a religion of slogans and soundbites, or ethics and morals? These are the questions of the hour. Yet the message in this volume is a message of hope. A repeated theme is that the beauty and richness of the Islamic tradition remains, and that if Muslims reclaim our ethical consciousness, testify to the truth, and stand for justice, then God will be with us. May the present collection set a new standard for Muslims moving forward. May God accept.

ॐ

The method used in editing the *khutbah*s should be explained. Editing is a highly subjective process. There were predictable problems in deciding what to keep, delete, and rearrange. Each *khutbah* presented its own challenges. Instances of repetition were typically abridged or deleted or, in a small number of cases, preserved for rhetorical effect. In several *khutbah*s, I restructured the order of paragraphs to fully bring out the ideas conveyed therein. What I have tried to achieve for readers is a clear and accessible text that retains, as much as possible, the very words used by Professor Abou El Fadl and that preserves his authentic style, tone, and voice. The hope is that readers can hear the Professor and the original *khutbah*s in the text, while still finding the written prose clear, easy to follow, and engaging.

Lastly, I am thankful to all those who helped in the publication of this volume. The Usuli Institute's vibrant community, online and in-person, was a bedrock of support throughout. I am especially indebted to Rami Koujah and Rameen Javadian, who significantly raised the quality of the finished text. I am also grateful to Grace Song, who entrusted me with this project and carried the work through to final publication. Finally, I must thank Professor Abou El Fadl himself, for reminding me—and surely many others—of what a just, beautiful, and ethical Islam looks like, and for demonstrating what a real *khutbah* is all about.

DR. JOSEF LINNHOFF
December 2021

A Note on Presentation

· · · · · · · · · · · · ·

$\mathcal{M}$any of the *khutbah*s contained in this volume were delivered before the process of collecting and editing *The Prophet's Pulpit* began. The following is a list of general editorial guidelines that have been followed throughout to impose a degree of structure and uniformity upon the text. Key concerns have included presentation, ease of reading, and preserving the tone and spirit of the original *khutbah*s while assisting readers not familiar with Arabic.

Professor Abou El Fadl often cites from the Qur'an in the original Arabic before explaining or paraphrasing—but not translating—the verse or passage in English. In such cases, translations are taken from *The Study Quran* (New York: HarperOne, 2015) and indicated in the text by "SQ." Instances where Professor Abou El Fadl offers his own translation of the Qur'an are indicated by "Q."

The intermittent use of Arabic terms is largely preserved but, in most cases, an English translation is inserted in parentheses after the first mention. For example: "*khutbah* (sermon)." Arabic terms that have become part of the English language or that defy simple translation, such as *jihad*, *Sunna*, or *hijab*, are not followed by parentheses. This involves a degree of subjectivity as to which terms are considered as such. All Arabic terms are included in the Glossary of Terms.

Professor Abou El Fadl occasionally expresses an idea or a turn of phrase in *both* English and Arabic. For ease of reading, in these cases, English has been preferred. In a small number of cases, the corresponding Arabic term has been included in parentheses.

The transliteration system avoids diacritics and includes *'ayn* and *hamza*.

Blessings that traditionally accompany the mention of both the Prophet and God, such as "peace be upon him" (*salla 'llahu 'alayhi wa-sallam*), both in English and Arabic, are omitted.

Anglicized names for the prophets have been chosen, i.e., Abraham, Moses, and Jesus, not Ibrahim, Musa, and 'Isa. In the same vein, the Anglicized "God" has been chosen over *Allah*.

Anglicized plurals have been chosen, i.e., *fatwa*s over *fatawa*, also *imam*s, *hadith*s.

Dates are given in the Islamic *Hijri* and then Common Era format. Dates of death are included after the mention of key historical figures from the Islamic intellectual tradition to offer further context.

Footnotes have been deliberately kept to a minimum. The exceptions are to cite *hadith* reports, further explain background context that may elude readers, and provide links to relevant secondary materials.

All Usuli Institute content cited in the footnotes can be found at the Usuli Institute's YouTube page: https://www.youtube.com/c/TheUsuliInstitute.

The spelling of Arabic terms largely follows that found in Professor Abou El Fadl's book, *The Search for Beauty in Islam: A Conference of the Books* (Oxford: Rowman & Littlefield, 2006). The same applies for both the Glossary of Terms and the Selected Biographies.

ᶾᵕ

INTRODUCTION

· · · · · · · · · · · ·

$\mathcal{F}$or any thinking person, there is perhaps no greater struggle than sitting through a mind-numbing *khutbah*, week in and week out. Over time, these experiences deflate the spirit, oppress the mind, and deaden the soul. They leave people in doubt about their faith.

Imagine if *khutbah*s could melt hearts, actually teach something new and inspiring from our vast tradition, and provide penetrating commentaries on the world we live in? Imagine if they addressed the real problems that Muslims confront? Imagine if they provided the knowledge to not just defend against Islamophobic rhetoric, but to make Muslims proud to be Muslim?

It is hard to imagine if one has never experienced that kind of *khutbah*. Do they actually exist? We believe so. They have been taking place at The Usuli Institute, and we present twenty-two such examples in this inaugural volume, the first of many, God willing (*insha'Allah*).

Khaled Abou El Fadl teaches us that every pulpit in Islam since the Prophet has been symbolically the pulpit of the Prophet,[1] and that to speak from the Prophet's pulpit is to indeed assume a very

---

1 The Usuli Institute, *The Prophet's Pulpit* (*Khutbah*, 16 October 2020).

heavy responsibility. It is a sanctified position, and the speaker owes that pulpit a diligent search for truth, justice, and superior knowledge—that which far exceeds common knowledge. Professor Abou El Fadl reminds us that there is a trust—a moral obligation between the speaker and the congregation—that the speaker will testify honestly about what is most serious and compelling for their lives as Muslims. If one is unable to meet this standard, they should not step on the pulpit. The title of this volume is intended as a reminder that those who stand on the Prophet's pulpit are following in the footsteps of the Prophet.

Most striking is just how far our modern-day reality has fallen from this standard. And yet few deliver on that standard quite like Khaled Abou El Fadl. In the coming pages, the reader is immediately transported to another world—a world of enlightenment, ethics, critical analysis, and humanity in all its complex forms—and how our God, our Qur'an, and our Prophet addressed the challenges of humankind. We are immersed in a world where *vibrant Islam* lives, and where the intellect, heart, and soul must live as one for a human to thrive. We learn how God's ethical trajectory for our faith arcs toward moral beauty, what that looked like at the Prophet's time, and what it should look like in ours. The message is deep, intuitive, and anchoring. It is at once liberating and empowering—and very foreign when compared to what Muslims experience at the mosque today. It demonstrates the vast disparity between an enlightened *khutbah* of a full-time scholar who has dedicated his life to studying a 1400-year-old tradition, and the *khutbah*s of countless doctors, engineers, board members, and others for whom reading books on Islam is a hobby. The latter have become the gatekeepers to the Prophet's pulpit to the grave detriment of the American Muslim experience in our times.

Over one year before American mosques were shuttered because of COVID-19, The Usuli Institute began offering virtual *khutbah*s.[2] We did so because we were convinced that the quality of *khutbah*s was so abysmally low, and the experience of going to the mosque had become so alienating for so many Muslims, particularly converts, women, and younger generations, that it became a religious duty to offer an alternative. Little did we know that in just over a year, our world would be transformed by a global pandemic and most everything would go virtual.

Meanwhile, the global condition of Muslims has continued its descent unabated. Our experience as Muslims in an Islamophobic world is largely confusing, painful, often hopeless, and wrought with doubt. In these dark times, there are few places to turn for an honest, educated voice that is dedicated to justice and grounded in the ethical tradition of Islam. There are even fewer if any scholars who are willing to speak truth to power, or able to connect the dots of injustice in the world, make it make sense, and bring it all back to what our tradition says about what our role as ethical Muslims should be.

Khaled Abou El Fadl does exactly that. Importantly, these virtual *khutbah*s quickly became a weekly commentary on our world from the lens of a distinguished scholar, thoroughly engaged in the problems of our age, while issuing uncomfortable wake-up calls to his beloved *Ummah*. Some readers may find this exposure unsettling. In the past, Professor Abou El Fadl has been accused of politicizing his *khutbah*s or "bringing politics to the pulpit." One could respond that silence is no less political. Or, one could note that calling for truth (*al-haqq*) and justice (*al-'adl*) is not political, only ethical. The

---

2 The Usuli Institute, *The Usuli Institute's First Virtual Khutbah*, (*Khutbah*, 25 January 2019). Also see Chapter 1: *The Usuli Institute's First Virtual Khutbah* in this volume.

present collection of *khutbah*s is "political" only if the Prophet was "political" when he challenged and condemned the unjust Meccan practices of his day.

What is undeniable in the pages that follow is the power of this education, and what resonates the loudest is the sound of truth. One feels the impact deep within, and there is a visceral cleansing effect for those searching for something greater, more beautiful, and more divine. It is our hope that by presenting these elevated *khutbah*s in book form, Muslims will recognize and demand a new standard worthy of the Prophet's pulpit in our times.

We are proud that this inaugural volume marks the first book published by Usuli Press, an imprint of The Usuli Institute. The Usuli Institute's mission is to elevate ethics, critical thinking, and dignity through education. We believe that the most important *jihad* of our times is the *jihad* of knowledge and ideas. Through this and future publications, we aim to leave a legacy of brave, thought-provoking, and inspiring work that is thoroughly grounded in our vast intellectual tradition, and that can liberate the mind, elevate the spirit, and unleash the divine potential in every human being. May God accept.

GRACE SONG
Executive Director
The Usuli Institute
January 2022

PART I

Foundations:
From
Darkness
to Light

1

The Usuli Institute's
First Virtual *Khutbah*

I start this *khutbah* (sermon) with a necessary explanation. It is not unusual for The Usuli Institute to hold *jumu'a* (Friday congregational prayer), but I take this opportunity to address the issue of *jumu'a* itself. God calls upon Muslims:

> *O you who believe! When you are called to the congregational prayer, hasten to the remembrance of God and leave off trade. That is better for you, if you but knew. (SQ 62:9)*

God calls upon believers to respond to the call to prayer at *jumu'a* by engaging in an act of *dhikr* (remembrance of God). It was an ongoing practice of the Prophet to hold *jumu'a* within the Muslim community. With the revelation of this verse, the Qur'an underscores that Muslims should leave their earthly affairs; if engaged in trade, business, or other affairs, they should set that aside and come together to remember God. Importantly, for those interested in the *fiqh* (jurisprudence) of *jumu'a*, it was never simply about a prayer of two *rak'ahs* (the prescribed units of prayer). It was an event that rekindled the faith and ignited a sense that the individual is connected to a collective, a nation, an *Ummah* (community of Muslims) that is, in turn, connected to God.

The mosque was the center of the Muslim community, a vibrant place in which all the important events took place. It was also at the heart of the decision-making process. In *jumu'a*, then, the remembrance of God was performed within a context of collective accountability. Often discussed at *jumu'a* were the most pressing affairs of the community. After the death of the Prophet, this tradition continued. The mosque remained a central cultural space in which Muslims discussed their affairs while remembering that their collective affairs are inherently and intimately tied to God. However, by the end of the Caliphate and the rise of the first Muslim dynasty, as happens in all authoritarian states, the Umayyads sought to control the space of *jumu'a*.[3] They sought to do so by pressuring jurists to agree to the idea that the state should appoint the *imam* (leader) that gives the *khutbah*. In so doing, the state sought to control that public space. The Umayyads and 'Abbasids would demand that a *du'a'* (supplication) be made during *jumu'a* for the ruler—"May God bless the ruler, may God protect the ruler"—and this continued into the Mamluk and Ayyubid eras in Syria and Egypt. We can talk at great length about this history, but what arose was a back and forth between the state that sought to control *jumu'a*, particularly the *khutbah* and *du'a'*, and acts of resistance that sought to reclaim *jumu'a* as belonging to the

---

3 An allusion to the transition of the seat of the Caliph and political authority to Damascus under Mu'awiya I in 41/661 after the death of the Prophet's cousin, son-in-law, and fourth Rightly Guided Caliph, 'Ali b. Abi Talib.

Muslim community, not the state. This centered on the question: who should decide the most qualified person to lead *jumuʿa*—the state or the judicial and jurisprudential institutions?

We know how the story proceeds in the modern age. Colonialism enters the scene. The first act of colonial powers, whether French, Dutch, or British, was to control *jumuʿa* and the *khutbah*, and to weaken the private institutions that educated, qualified, and certified jurists. After colonialism, mosques in the Muslim world fell under the ownership of the state. The state controls who becomes the *imam* of a mosque and even the content of the *khutbah* itself. And while it is clear from the *Sunna* of the Prophet that the *khutbah* is an integral and essential part of *jumuʿa*, since colonialism there has emerged a culture of apathy and disinterest. *Khutbah*s all over the Islamic world, due to their control by the state, have become irrelevant and marginal to public life. It has become common for Muslims to go to *jumuʿa* and daydream, think about everything else in the world, wait until the *khutbah* is over, do two prayers, and quickly leave. But this is not the spirit of *jumuʿa*. *Jumuʿa* is meant to be a spiritual renewal for the Muslim community. Once a week, we are meant to renew and reinvigorate, as a community, our commitment to God. We are meant to take account of what most concerns our community, and reflect, ponder, and make the end of the week, which was supposed to be *jumuʿa*, a crowning event of the remembrance of God.

My nature is to be extremely cautious whenever I break with established precedent. My nature is to respect the efforts of learned people before me. For twenty years, then, I resisted the idea of saying it is acceptable to join *jumuʿa* remotely. While jurisprudentially cautious, however, I know the matter is far more complicated than this. I will explain the reasons why shortly. The problem is that Muslims, as largely immigrants to the West, still carry the baggage, illnesses, and diseases from "back home" to their new lands. This is despite the fact that we no longer live under authoritarian states and can recreate the space that the Qur'an calls for. So *jumu'a* remains an uninspiring space for Muslims all over the world. For twenty years or more, I have noticed a consistent deterioration in the quality of *jumu'a*. This is a big topic but the basic reason for this is the problem of *imama* (leadership). There are rules for *jumu'a*. As mentioned earlier, jurists said that those leading *jumu'a* should be the most learned. If not, they should be those who are the most intimate with the Qur'an. But the "most learned" is a pressing criterion. The *Shari'a*, the path of God, is like a lantern, a beacon of light. That lantern can either be carried by a person who sees their way or by a blind person. The *Shari'a* remains a lantern, but who carries the *Shari'a*, the seeing or the blind?

Muslims in the West have lost touch with the *Shari'a*. They think a jurist is someone who memorizes the most Qur'an or *hadith*. They ignore that a true jurist not only knows the Qur'an and *Sunna* but is immersed in modern epistemology. What made jurists authoritative, compelling, and effective in the past was not their mastery of the raw material of law. Jurisprudence is to master the *application* of law, and that requires a great deal of learning and wisdom. As education systems for jurists have deteriorated, it has become very difficult to train a jurist in the modern world. So-called jurists today may have memorized a lot of Qur'an and *hadith*, but they are not trained in thinking and reason. They are not trained in causality or in basic ideas of obligation, duty, and responsibility. Most important of all, they are not trained in ethics, so they do not produce ethical law. It is like the blind man carrying the lantern; you go nowhere, for you are blind.

For over twenty years, I have witnessed many Muslims grow increasingly frustrated with *jumu'a*s in their local mosques. Many mosques rotate *khatib*s (speakers) who possess no specific credentials other than knowing the right people in the community. They are not the most knowledgeable, nor the most trained. They have no credentials other than having the right connections. Or they have memorized much of the Qur'an, like a tape recorder. As a result, the quality of *khutbah*s has declined and become alienating for many Muslims. Many stop attending *jumu'a* altogether or they attend but "zone out," listening to nothing, because there really is nothing to listen to. They quickly do their prayers and leave.

The Usuli Institute has held many *jumu'a*s before. Jurists disagree as to how many physical attendees are required for a valid *jumu'a*. Some say five, seven, or twenty, and others say more. But the crux of the issue is The Usuli Institute's invitation to those unable to be with us physically, to join us virtually.[4] Before explaining why I finally accepted this idea, let me take us on an interesting side note. Although the Qur'an says, "O believers, when you hear the call of *jumu'a*..." (Q 62:9), the vast majority of jurists, because of patriarchy and sexism, say that only men are obligated to attend *jumu'a*. In many parts of the Muslim world, women do not go to *jumu'a*. Yet that clearly contradicts the Qur'an's literal text and the practice of the early Muslims at the time of the Prophet, when most women attended *jumu'a*. We have cumulative reports about that. I also remember, when I was young in Kuwait, that several women complained that there was no available space in the mosques for them to attend *jumu'a*. Several *fatwa*s (non-binding legal opinions) advised

---

4 This *khutbah* was delivered in January 2019, one year before the start of the corona-virus pandemic. On the topic of virtual *khutbah*s during the pandemic, see Chapter 21: *Perhaps You Will Turn to God: On the Coronavirus and God's Love*, and Chapter 22: *More on Virtual* Khutbah*s and the Personal Nature of a Pandemic* in this volume.

them to follow *jumuʿa* on television and pray with the *imam*. This is an old *fatwa*. Those who think a virtual *jumuʿa* is new, then, are mistaken. It goes back to the 1950s and '60s. For decades, women have been praying *jumuʿa* virtually. And what is good for women is good for me. Do not tell me, "That is okay for women but not for men." We should grow up and stop thinking in this backward, unacceptable, and immoral way. Many have written to me who are ill or who cannot attend *jumuʿa*. Many women feel alienated and unwelcome in mosques. There are many who simply will not go to their local *jumuʿa* for the simple fact that they know enough about the religion. Not only do they find the *khutbah* alienating, but they know that some schools of Islamic law say that if the *imam* giving the *khutbah* and leading the prayer is not the most knowledgeable, the *jumuʿa* itself is invalid. Personally, I have a problem with that. If I go to *jumuʿa* and it is clear that the *imam* is far from qualified—and this has happened several times—I have a serious question as to whether my *jumuʿa* is valid. I pray *jumuʿa* with everyone and then I pray *Zuhr* (midday prayer) afterward.

The point is not to challenge or to compete with anyone. All those who are happy with their *imam* and *khutbah* should continue attending in person. It is always preferable to physically be with the community. But those unable to attend or who feel marginalized, disaffected, and who want a *khutbah* that brings them back to what is authentic and legitimate are welcome to follow this *jumuʿa*. That is how it should work. Let me say that Hanafi jurists have long held that the inhabitants of houses that surround a mosque may follow *jumuʿa* in their house so long as they can follow the *imam*, even if there is a wall between the mosque and house; in other words, as long as they can know whether the *imam* is in *sujud* (prostration) or *ruku'* (bowing). Maliki jurists have said that people can follow the *imam* in *jumu'a* even if there is a river or road separating them from the mosque. For Hanafis and Malikis, then, space is not the issue. The issue is that of correctly following the *imam*. Yet, there is ignorance in our age. There are those who claim that no one has ever said that you do not have to be physically present to follow *jumu'a*. This is simply not true. Hanafis and Malikis have talked about this for some time. Ironically, the most conservative on the issue are Shafi'is, and I am Shafi'i. But I break with my school here because, in my view, the point is not the correctness of the physical space, but the correctness of the act of remembrance of God in its totality. In other words, the point is the *khutbah* and the prayer and, if you can follow that, *jumu'a* is valid.

The irony is that modern technology, which, sadly, did not come from Muslim lands, but should have, enables us to do what Hanafis and Malikis rather progressively imagined well ahead of their time, that is, to follow the *imam* even though we are not physically present. Frankly, I am amazed by these jurists. There must have been some real case studies that enabled them to imagine this. In the days in which they were professionally trained, Muslim jurists exhibited a lot of impressive analytical thinking. Muslim jurists in our age often exhibit no thinking, let alone analytical thinking. Nevertheless, the substantive issue is that one can listen to the *khutbah* and correctly see what the *imam* is doing in the prayer. We can, of course, do this virtually and physically. Let me underscore: we compete with no one. We undermine no one. Those happy with their mosque community and leadership should continue to attend *jumu'a* in person. But those who know that there will be no remembrance of God must find an alternative. If this is an alternative for those who know they will listen to nothing in their local *khutbah*, but simply daydream about their bills or work, be impatient for the *khutbah* to finish, quickly pray, and depart, so be it.

I pray that my experience is not representative, but, sadly, I know it is. Over the course of thirty years, I have come to learn that the more knowledgeable and trained you are, the less access you have to the pulpit of *jumu'a* in Islamic centers in the U.S. Every month or two, I give a *khutbah* at the Islamic Center of Southern California (ICSC). I will continue doing so as long as they have me.[5] But Muslims must learn that nothing is more valued by God than honesty, and Muslims must learn to be honest when they talk. There is a problem when the more educated, trained, and knowledgeable you are, the more you threaten people who do not want you to stand on the pulpit. Most of these people have rich professional lives. They are doctors, engineers, and businessmen. But they do not want someone competing with their extracurricular activity. God knows this is not something I covet, but I have finally acceded to all the demands, emails, and requests to have a regular *khutbah* in addition to those at the ICSC. My hope and prayer is to bring solace to all those who currently do not find solace and guidance in their *jumu'a*s.

Jumu'a should leave you with something that hearkens the remembrance of God in your heart. I leave you with this. In a *hadith* that is not often heard in the modern age, the Prophet praises those who are consistent in the remembrance of God. The Prophet

---

5 This collaboration with the ICSC ended in June 2019 following the decision of the ICSC to ban Professor Abou El Fadl from delivering the Friday *khutbah* after his suggestion to perform *janaza* (funerary) prayers for President Muhammad Morsi, the slain democratically elected leader of Egypt, and after censoring him from speaking about the associated injustices taking place in Egypt. This act of censoring, the refusal to stand up for justice, and the justification of such immoral behavior mirrors the authoritarianism and despotism that is rampant in the Muslim world. See The Usuli Institute, *On Being Banned: Shaming or Schooling the ICSC?* (*Khutbah*, 21 June 2019).

says that this group, which he calls *"al-Mutanazzihun,"* are lit up
by this remembrance; the first thing God does is put light in their
hearts; when that light ignites their hearts, they come to know God
as God knows them.[6] God is the light of the heavens and the earth.
The heavens and the earth are otherwise dark matter, anti-matter.
The only affirmative beauty is the light of God. If you are among
al-Mutanazzihun, the remembrance of God becomes a consistent part
of your existence. God ignites light in your heart so that you have
knowledge of God as God has knowledge of you. Can you imagine
a more intimate and beautiful relationship? Is it not something to
aspire for? Is it not something to make all your troubles wash away?
"God, let me know You as You know me." What more could one
want? Ask yourself: do I reflect light? Do I exhibit the light of the
Divine everywhere I go and in everything I do? Or do I reflect
darkness, boredom, or paleness? If you have the light of God, you
exhibit the light of God. The light of God does not make people sad.
It does not hurt people. It does not make people suffer. It does not
imprison people, torture people, or make people cry in despair. The
light of God makes people happy. If you have and reflect that light,
that will be your state and your affair. I leave you with that message.

25 January 2019

---

6 Abu Hamid al-Ghazali, *Ihya' 'Ulum al-Din* (Jedda: Dar al-Minhaj li-l-Nashr
wa-l-Tawzi', 2011), 5/78. The same report is found with slightly different wording in
al-Tirmidhi (3596).

2

On Evaluating Moral Character, Trusting Intuition, and Cleaning Your Vessel

O mankind! Verily there has come unto you a proof from your Lord. And We have sent down unto you a clear light. As for those who believe in God and hold fast to Him, He will cause them to enter into His Mercy and Bounty, and will guide them unto Himself upon a straight path. (SQ 4:174-5)

The words of the Qur'an bring consolation and guidance to our hearts. The words of the Qur'an will continue to resonate throughout the ages, calling upon our innate nature and intuitive senses. In these verses, God tells us that we have been given clear proof from our Lord, meaning clear signposts, a clear method, and a clear message. We have also been given a light, something luminous that can differentiate right from wrong, pure from impure, clean from unclean, moral from immoral. Mercy and compassion will be granted to those who hold steadfast to the Lord. In an act of grace, they will be guided to the Lord.

If the words of the Qur'an fall upon a pure heart, few words are needed to ignite the path of truth in that person. No great elaborations or discourses are needed, only the simple call that this is the path of light. It is like clean water. If poured into a clean vessel, it is a source of life and nourishment. If poured into an unclean vessel, however, it becomes a source of destruction, poison, and harm. When the Qur'an says that it addresses our *fitra* (intuition, Q 30:30), it assumes that we have worked on purifying our intuition and keeping our intuition healthy and robust. This is precisely why a psychotic, diseased, or impure intuition will not be transformed by the mere fact of the Qur'an being recited. A diseased intuition narcissistically absorbs everything to legitimate and justify itself and itself alone. It will do precisely this with the words of the Qur'an, gaining nothing from its revelation. An intuition that is healthy and pure, however, will take the Qur'an and elevate itself with it.

This is the nature of the created word. Words are powerful. The same words used to praise the Lord and build a relationship with God are those that people with diseased hearts use for nefarious purposes. This revelation is a gateway to either the best or the worst of ourselves. It is for this reason that Imam 'Ali, in one of his famous teachings, says, "When you hear a transmission," meaning when you hear a report attributed to the Prophet, "receive it with your reflective intellect. Do not evaluate it simply through its chain of transmission." He then adds, "Those who transmit knowledge (*'ilm*)," meaning those who only memorize and parrot knowledge, repeating it like recorders, "are many. But those capable of studying and evaluating knowledge are few."[7] In another famous report, Imam 'Ali says that a true jurist does not make people despair of God's mercy nor alienate people from the spirit and light of God.[8]

I received so many messages in response to my previous *khutbah*.[9] So many are in a state of anxiety and worry. They ask, "How can we be expected to rely on our intellect and intuition? Are you saying that we should throw out all the scholarship that comes from countries of despotism and hypocrisy?" Let me be clear. I am not saying that one should throw away everything. I am simply saying what the Prophet said, namely, that the backbone of a Muslim is their sense of reason, rationality, and intellect. The Prophet said that our greatest authority is the heart, not *Shaykh* so-and-so. Listen to knowledge. Seek knowledge. Pursue knowledge. But also assess where knowledge comes from. Assess the moral character of your teacher. If your teacher is in bed with the powerful and participates in the oppression of others, aiding and abetting despots, then it is your duty to investigate your sources. That is what a rational human being does. Secondly, you cannot divorce a human being from their conduct. If your teacher is aloof or refuses to get their hands dirty with the mechanisms of oppression and despotism, then they are probably someone you can trust. If your teacher is in bed with oppressors and despots, however, you should be cautious. In fact, you should be skeptical of anything that comes out of their mouth.

It is a matter of credibility. Assessing credibility is a conscientious obligation upon every Muslim. You will be responsible before God

---

7 Imam 'Ali b. Abi Talib, *Nahjul Balagha* (Potomac, MD: Ahlul Bayt Assembly of America, 1417/1996), 275.

8 Ibid., 273.

9 See Chapter 11: *Recolonization, Racism, and the Role of Reason* in this volume.

for your failure to be conscientious when there was a reason to be so. Imagine saying to God on the Final Day, "I relied upon *Shaykh* such-and-such," and God responds, "Did you not know that he helped in the oppression of people? Did you not know that he was unjust?" If you are deemed negligent in your obligation to know, you will be held to account. This is common sense. It is the same reason (*'aql*) that God has granted, endowed, and ingrained in each of us. We do not dismiss any scholarship. In evaluating scholarship, however, we evaluate the text, the context of the text, the transmitter of the text, and their track record. We know we do not have the time to become scholars ourselves. The least we can do is be conscientious in choosing which scholars we take as figures of authority in our life.

Use the gift that God gave you. Remember that every intellect is unique and that this is part of the miracle of diversity that God has created. Had God willed, people would not be different. God created them to be different (Q 10:99; 13:31; 35:28). The fact you think in ways that do not mirror others is no bad thing. It is what creates richness. It is proof of Divinity. This is why the Prophet said the most secure people in the Hereafter are the most thoughtful in the here and now.[10] I repeat it because of how unusual it is for modern Muslims, sadly, to hear that thinking and reflecting are Islamic obligations. They are a solemn obligation that you are rewarded for. If you are not a thinking and reflective human being, then you are a robot that mechanically follows habits and traditions without reflecting upon what is just and unjust, beautiful and ugly, humane and inhumane. You will be held responsible for that in the Hereafter.

"But how can I trust my intellect and intuition?" This is the obvious question. First, develop your relationship with God. At a

---

10 Al-Ghazali, *Ihya'*, 1/282.

minimum, pray, fast, and face God. If you do not even do this, you do not have a relationship that will allow you to evaluate and filter Islamic knowledge. You may be able to filter secular knowledge. If you seek to evaluate Islamic knowledge, however, meaning the Qur'an, *Sunna*, and *fiqh*, this is the alphabet. These are the rules of the game. Second, make your tongue moist with the remembrance of God. The more we remember God, the more our intuition and intellect reaches a position to evaluate things from a perspective that is Islamically comfortable, serene, and tranquil. Third, never assume that you know. All you can say is, "In my position, this does not sit well with my conscientious thinking. And I cannot perform something that does not sit well with my conscientious thinking." So, work on your prayer, build a relationship with God, and take a conscientious pause. Do not tell others what God wants them to do, but in your own affairs, take account of your individual autonomy and sovereignty. You cannot do something unless your intellect and heart are persuaded. Do not force them into persuasion. Be honest enough to say, "I do not buy this. It does not make sense to me. I will continue praying on it." That is all you can do. It is no one else's business. You have the right to tell people, "This is between me and God."

The Prophet said that if you do not even recognize evil, then you are in serious trouble. This is the most important thing. It is when one sees genocide, for example, and their heart does not even move. All people, of all faiths and races, recognize genocide. God has endowed in all human beings some primordial knowledge regardless of language, culture, or religion. These are the basic norms of morality that must, at a minimum, speak to the heart. If this is not the case, we are in serious trouble. If you see refugees starving and freezing, or refugee children dying or being trafficked, and you go to bed every night and never think of them, you are in trouble. If you never think of the children separated from their parents at the border and lost in the system, many of whom end up in foster care or trafficked into pedophile rings, you are in trouble. If you read these stories and your heart is untroubled, you have a problem. This is why the Prophet said that the kernel of a person is that their heart recognizes right from wrong. All the Islamic knowledge, *fiqh*, and Qur'an memorization in the world will avail you nothing if you can read that young people were tortured into confession and executed, as happened recently in Egypt, and it does not bother you. I can tell you that all your *fiqh* and theology are worthless. Before anything, we are moral human beings. If you read that a person was deceived, assassinated, and had his body dissolved in acid, and you ask, "What is the big deal?" then all the knowledge in the world is worthless.[11] You are a dirty vessel.

Pour clear water into a dirty vessel and the water becomes dirty in turn. You need to develop a sense of morality to clean your vessel so that the purified water of the Qur'an can enter your heart, invigorate your soul, and transform your life. Without that purification and basic sense of morality, it is a non-starter. There is no doubt that as Muslims we are going through trying times. But what was first compromised was our collective ethical conscience. In my theological outlook, the loss of an ethical conscience takes one out of the field of receiving God's grace, aid, and blessings.

I will give you one example. We know what happened to Bosnian Muslims in the 1990s. I refer to the genocide, rape camps, and suffering. At the time, we said, "Never again." But Islamophobia exploded and we now have the genocide against the Rohingya

---

11 An allusion to the murder of Saudi journalist Jamal Khashoggi in the Saudi consulate in Istanbul on 2 October 2018.

Muslims, which is perhaps even more horrific. But because the Rohingyas are of Bengali origin and dark skinned, no one cares. Because they are skinny and resemble the maids that work in the Gulf, no one cares. That is the sad truth. Consider, too, the fate of the Uyghur Muslims, who are among the oldest Muslim communities in the world with an amazingly rich culture and intellectual and ethical tradition. Uyghur writings on the relationship between Islam and Buddhism are mind-boggling and beautiful. The Chinese government has started to gather them in concentration camps, called "re-education camps," in which hundreds if not thousands are tortured and perish.[12] There are horrendous reports that Rohingya and Uyghur Muslims are prohibited from practicing Islam. They are not allowed to pray. Their mosques are torn down. Their families have been separated. Yet, we have an Islamophobe as President so the White House does not care.[13]

If we can at least understand Donald Trump's bigotry and racism, how do we make sense of the symbolic leader of the Muslim world, the so-called "Guardian of the Holy Sites," the Crown Prince, Muhammad Bin Salman (MBS)? MBS traveled to China and, when asked about the plight of Uyghur Muslims, said, "China has the right to protect itself from terrorism and extremism."[14] What most interests me is the Saudi religious establishment. In the face of the extermination of millions of Muslims in China, MBS's clerics say,

---

12 Note the date of this *khutbah* in March 2019. As of December 2021, it is widely reported that the number of Uyghur Muslims held in detention in Chinese camps numbers in the millions. Reports of rape, extra-judicial murder, torture, and organ harvesting are widespread. For more see The Usuli Institute, *The Tyranny of the Nervous System and the Muslim Betrayal of Uyghur Muslims* (*Khutbah*, 11 June 2021), and *The Meaning of Hajj and the Uyghur Holocaust* (*Khutbah*, 16 July 2021).

13 A reference to then-U.S. President, Donald Trump.

14 A reference to comments made by Muhammad Bin Salman on a state visit to China in February 2019. The comments were widely reported by news media outlets at the time.

"Wonderful!" There are Muslims who tell me that a cleric from Saudi Arabia has told them to wear the *hijab*. My first response is to ask, "Why do you even listen to this cleric? Why do you care what he says?" Regardless of what he says—wear *hijab*, do not wear *hijab*, do this, do that—this is someone who aids unjust rulers. They have no credibility. They cannot speak to you in good conscience.

This is what I am calling for. It is not rocket science. It is basic morality. Ask your heart: would the Prophet look at the murder of someone like Jamal Khashoggi and say, "That is Islam"? If you believe so, why are you Muslim? In that case, to be a Muslim would be an immoral thing. Would the Prophet say it is okay to exterminate millions of Muslims in China? Would the Prophet ignore the genocide against the Rohingya? Would the Prophet say it is okay to torture a group of innocent twenty-year-olds, convict them, and put them to death for a crime? Would the Prophet agree with Egypt's *Dar al-Ifta' al-Misriyya* issuing a *fatwa* that says, in effect, "It does not really matter whether they were guilty or not because we must fight the Muslim Brotherhood"?[15] Is that the religion of Muhammad? If your answer is "Yes" to any of these questions, then it is immoral to be a Muslim. That is what I cannot stand for.

I close with this. From among his many valuable teachings, Imam 'Ali says that a true *imam* must first educate themselves before aspiring to educate others; they should start by building their own ethical being and set an example in action, not words.[16] Imam 'Ali says a teacher of the self is more worthy of admiration than someone who teaches others. The highest form of teaching is the teaching of

---

15 *Dar al-Ifta' al-Misriyya* is an Egyptian Islamic advisory, judiciary, and governmental body established as a center for Islam and Islamic legal research in Egypt. It purports to offer Muslims religious guidance and advice through the issuing of *fatwas* on contemporary issues.

16 'Ali b. Abi Talib, *Nahjul Balagha*, 271.

the self. If you want to assess any *imam*, teacher, or scholar, look at their conduct. Look at their moral orientation. Do they start with themselves or with others? Do they find faults in themselves before finding faults in others? Are they endowed with that beautiful aura of humility and shyness, or are they arrogant and aggressive? Are they eager to put their own self in its place? Or are they eager to put others in their place? Do they more often claim knowledge or admit ignorance? Are they, first and foremost, educators of themselves? Are they obsessed with seeking knowledge or with spewing out knowledge? Do you often see them studying or blabbing?

If you see humility, shyness, and the seeking of knowledge, Imam ʿAli tells us that this is someone you should not blindly follow, but who is worthy of your respect and an assumption of credibility until proven otherwise. If they are in fact the opposite, such an *imam* is not worthy of your respect. They do not deserve an assumption of credibility. The assumption, in fact, should be the opposite. Such a person does not possess even the basics to qualify as an *imam*, jurist, or teacher. This is not because of their qualifications. It is because of their conduct. Consider the *imam* who, regardless of how much Qur'an he recites, marries and abuses women, treating them as if they are a commodity. Shame on you if you learn a single word from him. Shame on you. That *imam* has simply no moral character. When he learns how to treat women, we can then talk about what he knows. If he does not know how to treat women, however, then he can be my accountant. He can even be my lawyer. But he cannot be my *imam*.

1 March 2019

3

On Reading and Testing the State of Your Faith

$\mathcal{M}$odern Muslims often ignore the rather obvious point that all the prophets of God, without exception, were a voice for the dispossessed against the empowered. All the prophets came to the oppressed (*al-mustad'afun*). They spoke for the oppressed against the oppressor. This theme is basic and consistent to monotheism. It is the same message that God has repeatedly sent, time and again, with every prophet.

One of the major disagreements that we as Muslims have with the Old Testament is that it describes the prophets as sometimes indulging in the sins of power. Many stories in the Old Testament frame the prophets, such as David and Solomon, as having become sufficiently empowered as to commit injustices and transgress upon the rights of others. Islam completely rejects that narrative. Muslims must understand the political role of the Prophet in Medina as that of an exemplary ruler who ruled with absolute justice and an unwavering commitment to empower the disempowered. As a leader and ruler, the Prophet Muhammad governed by moral precepts and a strict ethical paradigm. People fell in love with the Prophet because of his mercy, compassion, justice, social empathy, and uncorrupted character.

Another critical lesson is that Muslims at the time of the Prophet would enter into a covenant with him in which it was stated that they must continue to speak for truth. Even in the presence of the Prophet, they would not surrender their free will. While the Qur'an tells Muslims to obey God and the Prophet (Q 3:32), this did not require Muslims to relinquish their right to speak for justice and to defend principles. In other words, following the Prophet did not mean erasing their own heart and personality.

If Muslims would reflect on that lesson, it would solve so many pedantic issues. It would remind us that our conscience must be sharp, lively, and active. This is essential to our moral agency on behalf of God. At no point are we as Muslims allowed to dull our conscience and simply say, "We follow orders." This moral agency is what distinguishes the message of the Qur'an from Christianity, especially pre-Islamic and medieval Christianity, in which a person's moral agency was surrendered to the Church. It also distinguishes the Qur'an from pre-Islamic and medieval Judaism in which moral agency was surrendered to the Rabbinic class. That is why the Qur'an criticizes the role of the Rabbinic class (Q 2:79; 4:46; 5:63; 9:30-31).

It is time for Muslims to rethink the ways we have lost and surrendered our moral agency. It is time for us to engage in self-reform and self-revision. The Qur'an and our Islamic tradition are clear about the role of moral agency. But we often act as if we can surrender our moral agency to injunctions written in a book. We think it is enough to read a *hadith* and let that become the bearer of our moral agency; beyond that, we do not have to worry. This is extremely dangerous because without moral agency we are not real believers. It is like when the unbelievers ask God to send an angel:

> *And they would say, "Why has not an angel been*
> *sent down unto him?" Had We sent down an*
> *angel, then the matter would be decreed, and*
> *they would be granted no respite. (SQ 6:8)*

The Qur'an responds that had God sent an angel, it would be all over. Why? Because the act of moral agency and voluntariness would then become meaningless. You cannot disbelieve in a physical presence like an angel. God tells us that we have been given moral agency. With that moral agency, we are free to believe or not.

Even after attaining belief, however, there remains the challenges of hypocrisy and *shirk* (associating partners with God). Manifest *shirk* (*shirk jalli*) is to claim that God has a son or that there are two gods. Hidden *shirk* (*shirk khafi*) is to worship money over God in the heart. Hypocrisy is stealthy. We are all hypocrites. We are often hypocritical with our families, friendships, and jobs. We say something but do something different. We expect from others what we do not expect from ourselves. These are all forms of hypocrisy. Moral agency is critical.

We have also learned from previous *khutbah*s that the nature of tyrants and oppressors is to accuse their opponents of the worst crimes. Pharaoh accuses Moses of being a terrorist (Q 40:26). As a Muslim, do you sympathize with the powerful against the disempowered? Do you believe the powerful when they accuse the disempowered of the ugliest crimes, as Pharaoh accused Moses? This is also part of the challenge of moral agency. If this is the case, then there is something wrong. There is something wrong in your spirit, intellect, and in your understanding of the faith.

In this *khutbah*, we will add another element to this critical understanding of our faith. It relates to one of the most awe-inspiring passages in the Qur'an:

> *Whomsoever God wishes to guide, He expands his breast*
> *for submission. And whomsoever He wishes to lead*
> *astray, He makes his breast narrow and constricted,*
> *as if he were climbing to the sky. Thus does God heap*
> *defilement upon those who do not believe. This is the*
> *path of thy Lord, made straight. We have expounded*
> *the signs for a people who take heed. (SQ 6:125-6)*

God describes those whose chests are narrow and constricted as like those "climbing to the sky" (SQ 6:125). In our modern age, we know that the more one rises, the less oxygen there is. Previous generations of commentators struggled to understand this verse. They did not know that there is less oxygen as one rises. The Qur'an is full of indicators that its author is aware of sciences that were discovered only centuries later.

The mark of faith is the feeling of repose and tranquility in the chest. The mark of straying from God is a feeling of angst. There is so much to say about a verse like this. Note that God points to the nature of Islam as repose, tranquility, and the removal of angst. The sign of a physical illness is an ache or a fever. The sign of a spiritual illness is a sense of angst and turbulence in the chest. What of those who claim to believe but have a constant state of angst in the chest? Think about this verse. God helps those whom God wishes to guide to Islam. God helps them so that there is repose and peace in their heart. God only helps those who help themselves (Q 13:11). It is not an error or a lottery system without reason or logic. That idea should be set aside. God does not play favorites for no reason. God is the Most Wise and the Most Just.

If you want to test the state of your faith, check your angst. How does your chest feel? If you are always anxious and worried, there is an illness in the relationship. There is a lack of trust in what God brings. People often deal with a sense of angst by resorting to drugs, alcohol, distractions, games, and sex. It is an illness and human beings respond to it. People also deal with angst by acquiring a lot of money and possessions. They belong to expensive clubs in which they waste tremendous amounts of money. Ultimately, however, God tells the Prophet that it is not up to him who will be guided (Q 2:213, 272; 24:35; 35:8; 39:23). If a Muslim hurts someone else because they are not a believer, or because they consider them a bad Muslim, that person has no guidance in their heart. This is a critical point. It is no doubt the sign of a lack of faith. For if God had willed, that person would have been truly guided. God tells us clearly that it is up to God.

Let me give an example. I recently learned about the producer of a documentary entitled *Fitna*, which was released after 9/11. It is a horrible piece of propaganda against Islam. The producer of the documentary, Arnoud van Doorn, has since become Muslim. He has spoken at length about his conversion. I was listening to his interviews and this verse (Q 6:125-6) kept repeating in my mind. He said his heart was full of angst after finishing the documentary. Then, upon simply deciding to read the Qur'an, his heart was full of tranquility. Such tranquility is a gift from God. It is as if God said, "You worked hard in hating me, but I love you. You read the Qur'an, so I will reward you by touching your heart." This is the same person that I saw in 2006 and thought, "What a devil." I watched his recent videos and said to myself, "His face is full of light. It is full of beauty. What a beautiful human being."

As a Muslim, ask God to fill your heart with that tranquility and repose. You will shine outwardly. Ask God to remove the angst in your heart, whether it is due to worries over your future, anger at your spouse, or because you have other problems. Angst is from the devil. Repose and peace are from the Divine.

I want to bring attention to another element in Surah al-An'am. Every Qur'anic chapter is full of wisdom. Each chapter has its own personality and forms part of an ethical totality. God says:

> And thus have We made great ones among the guilty in every
> town, that they may plot therein. But they only plot against
> themselves, though they are unaware. And when a sign comes
> unto them, they say, "We will not believe till we are given
> the like of that which was given to the messengers of God."
> God knows best where to place His message. Humiliation
> before God and a severe punishment shall soon befall the
> guilty for that which they used to plot. (SQ 6:123-4)

There are so many points to address in this verse. Yet there is one aspect of the verse that people do not usually notice. God tells us who poses the greatest danger to light and the biggest attraction to darkness. It is the "great ones among the guilty" (SQ 6:123). It is the powerful and rich who often have hearts full of angst. They often cause the most corruption. This does not simply mean that they are powerful, unfair, unjust, and oppressive. Rather, God points our attention to a critical point. It is that they say to the prophets, "We will not believe till we are given the like of that which was given to the messengers of God" (SQ 6:124). Most Muslims read this and think it means they are jealous of Muhammad and wonder why they were not chosen as prophets. Rich people are entitled. But this is not quite the meaning of the verse. The verse includes this, but it is not the critical point. The critical point is that the rich and powerful want the legislative and executive powers of the prophets of God. The source of their corruption is their haughtiness and arrogance. Even when they become believers, they effectively use the message of the prophets to empower themselves by demanding a doctrine of obedience in society. Look at every tyrant. Few tyrants seek to destroy the idea of God in society. Stalin is the exception. What is far more common is for tyrants to seek the legislative and executive powers of prophets. They embrace the religious establishment, but then demand obedience to themselves.

We find this among so many modern Muslims. They cite the verse: "Obey God, obey the Prophet and the rulers" (Q 4:59), as if obeying rulers is equal to obeying God and the Prophet. Rulers who usurp the power of God and the prophets, however, are the hallmark of an injustice that erases tranquility in the heart, teaches people hypocrisy, and creates a heaviness in the chest. This is what happens when you teach people the doctrine of so-called "Madkhali" and "Jami" Islam. These two schools of thought are now supported by all Muslim countries, rich and poor, and teach the doctrine of obedience to the extent that even if the ruler commands something against God or the Prophet, one must still obey. The only paradigm in society is that of obedience to the ruler.

In an authoritarian country like Egypt, for example, you can appear on television and say the most awful things about the Prophet. You can trash the Companions. You can trash the Qur'an. You can trash Islamic history as backward, reactionary, and retarded. But you cannot criticize the President of Egypt, 'Abdul Fattah al-Sisi. I recently saw an interview with Nawal El Saadawi, an Egyptian feminist, in which she gave a long and horrible lecture about how we should be able to criticize the Qur'an and *Sunna*.[17] Fine—I agree. But the interviewer then asked if she would criticize Sisi. Saadawi had a fit, and the interviewer was fired. In Syria, you can say whatever you want about the *Sunna* and Companions. You can trash them. You can say, "I am a secularist" or "I am an atheist." But you cannot say a word about the ruler, Bashar al-Assad. This is precisely what the Qur'an is warning us about: the rich and powerful demand the authority of prophets. If you cannot keep prophetic authority distinct from human authority, then illness will inevitably inhabit your heart.

The same applies for Donald Trump. Some Muslims have written to me, saying, "We must obey Trump because God ordered us to cooperate with even unjust rulers." When you allow the doctrine of obedience to prevail over your moral agency, you allow a despot to become your effective god. The problem is not one of obedience itself. I obey the law as an American citizen. But I obey the law as an institution in which I partake. My allegiance is to the law, not the President. For the law represents a symbol of justice. My real boss, however, other than the law, is God and the Prophet. I do not give my moral agency to anyone. When you pledge to obey a human being without exercising moral agency, it is as if you have given an oath of allegiance but did not agree, like the Companions, to stand for truth. Remember that the Companions made an oath to obey the Prophet but to also stand for truth. Even with the Prophet, they would not surrender their moral agency. So how about with those who are not prophets?

---

17 For more on Nawal El Saadawi, see The Usuli Institute, *On Nawal El Saadawi, Alhurra channel, and the Limits of Free-thinking* (*Khutbah*, 26 March 2021).

This is what the enemies of Islam use to plant doubts in our youth. They tell our children that the religion of their parents is backward and retarded. The Prime Minister of Great Britain, Boris Johnson, has a book on Rome, which I know Muslims will not have read, because Muslims do not read—that is the problem.[18] In the book, Johnson talks about Islam and cites Winston Churchill, praising Churchill's understanding of the Muslim world, particularly his view that the problem with the Muslim world is Islam itself; Islam is a despotic religion that prevents its followers from understanding the basics of liberty. Who does Johnson rely on? He relies on our idiotic Muslim brothers and sisters who teach the doctrine of obedience. God warns us that the most corrupt are the rich and powerful, who seek an authority co-equal to the prophets. God warns us not to surrender our moral agency for it will benefit us nothing in the Hereafter. We will not be able to say in the Hereafter, "I did this because Trump, Sisi, Assad, Muhammad Bin Salman (MBS), or Muhammad Bin Zayed (MBZ) told me to." It will avail us nothing. Islam is the religion of grave, meticulous moral agency. We should teach that to our children.

So much happens every week. There is no hope of touching upon even a little of what is relevant. But several things have caught my attention and are worth raising. A U.S. citizen named Reem Mohammed El-Desoky recently went to Egypt. She has been living in the United States for many years. Her twelve-year-old son was born in the U.S. El-Desoky went to Egypt, was stopped at the airport upon her arrival, and arrested. Why? Because she had posted reports on Facebook about human rights abuses in Egypt. The Egyptian

18 Boris Johnson, *The Dream of Rome* (London: Harper Perennial, 2007). Note that the final chapter on Islam in the book is covered under "Part Four: What Went Wrong," and entitled, "And Then Came the Muslims."

government detained her in the airport for eighteen hours, separating her from her child. They then took her to an unknown location. The child was handed to another American-Egyptian family in Egypt, who flew him back to the U.S.

This bothers me not just as a Muslim but as an American citizen. The woman disappears. No one knows where she is. Eventually, it is confirmed that she is being charged with belonging to the Muslim Brotherhood (MB) and spreading false news about Egypt. There is no evidence that she has anything to do with the MB. She has only posted on Facebook about human rights violations in Egypt. Yet, there is no independent judiciary in Egypt and she will be convicted like everyone else who is charged on similar grounds. Imagine the devastation upon this poor family, the poor twelve-year-old, and his poor mother. Once again, however, the only people speaking about this are non-Muslim human rights organizations. For the most part, Muslims are silent. It is as if the amount of ugliness in their lives has rendered them immune to shock or offense. When they become like this, however, they are no longer true Muslims.

I have been reading about Christian evangelism and missionary work in the Muslim world. One of the first things Muslim children learn from evangelists is to look at the amount of injustice committed by Muslims against Muslims. They tell our children, "Do you ever hear your parents react? Do you ever hear them outraged?" The child says, "They never talk about it. They avoid these topics." The evangelist replies, "This is because in Islam it is not considered bad. In Islam, it is okay to frame and arrest people."

When are Muslims going to wake up? Do you know who are the biggest defenders of Sisi, MBS, and MBZ? It is the right-wing fascist Benjamin Netanyahu and his Israeli government. Who praised Sisi's "great wisdom" and came to the defense of the Islamic

Center of Southern California (ICSC) after my fall out with them?[19] Islamophobic organizations, including the *Clarion Project*. It should speak volumes when people who hate Islam attack someone who speaks about justice and human rights, and praise Muslims who are silent about injustice, suffering, and oppression. If this does not awaken you or bring some life into your moral conscience, then there is no hope. Reflect on this. It should be a moment of education and deep reflection. Those who hate Islam celebrate every time Muslims confront injustice with silence. Those who hate Islam celebrate when only non-Muslim countries come to the aid of Muslims in China and many Muslim countries even support the oppression. How does this reach our children? "Look at this loser religion. Look at the religion of your parents. They stand by injustice. They do not even care about their own kind."

I know that the Islam that I believe in and teach is the only true Islam. I say this without a shadow of a doubt. The Islam that condones concentration camps for fellow Muslims is false. The Islam that hands over political asylees, as both Qatar and Kuwait recently did to Saudi Arabia, is false. The Islam that oppresses and arrests people for criticizing a ruler is false. If Reem El-Desoky was cursing the Prophet on Facebook, like many Egyptians these days, no one would have touched her. You can curse God and the Prophet, but you cannot curse Sisi: that is a false Islam. You will not be able to raise your head in front of your children unless you declare very openly, with me, that this is not real Islam. Your children will not grow to respect you because you are not a role model. You are a moral coward. Children will never respect moral cowards.

19 See footnote 3.

Reem El-Desoky is in prison suffering. She will raise her hands to supplicate to God. Know that God hears the *du'a'* of the oppressed. Know that God will punish those who remain silent. When your children grow up and they are not Muslim, and you ask, "Why, God?", remember this. Remember how you left Reem El-Desoky and her suffering twelve-year-old and did not even support her with a tweet. You did not even support her in your heart. I do not know her. I have never met her. But I looked at her file. She has nothing to do with the MB. She never had. Anyone opposing a ruler these days in the Muslim world is accused of being MB, and, by implication, a terrorist.

I will close with a heart-warming story. You do not see real Islam or the beauty of Islam in the annals of power, authority, and oppression. Idlib in Syria is being bombed and its civilians are slaughtered daily by the Russian and Syrian governments. Out of this immense suffering, Grace, my wife, introduced me to a group on Facebook called *Little Hearts Cuoricini*. This group is amazing. They shelter and feed orphans whose parents have been killed in the conflict. They do this with the total conviction that what they do is for the sake of God. They not only shelter and feed orphans. They also sing, dance, and draw with them. They put smiles on faces. In addition, as they were rescuing orphans amid the rubble, they found a kitten that was ill and suffering. In an act of amazing beauty, they saved the kitten and took it to a vet. The comment by one of the brave men on the video broke my heart. He holds the kitten, and says, "The Prophet taught us that if you save a life, you save the entire earth." There, in Idlib, amid the suffering and rubble, we see what Islam means. "The bombs are falling on my head, but I dedicate my life to teach children the alphabet while dancing, singing, and drawing with them, and saving suffering animals on the streets."

That is the real Islam. That is the true Islam.

This man's heart, I assure you, despite the death and suffering, is one of repose, tranquility, and comfort. Not angst. Not anxiety. This is the true Islam. It is not the Islam of Sisi, MBS, and MBZ. The reason I mention them is so that you can look them up. Donate money. Save your soul. If they are doing their part, God will hold you responsible for the suffering of these orphans in the Hereafter. They have offered you a way out. I have never met them. I do not know them. Support those taking care of suffering orphans and animals. That is the manifestation of true Islam. Show them that you can be a true Muslim too.

26 July 2019

4

Knowing the Strength of Your Inner Light

The Prophet would often repeat a *du'a'* that, like so many of his supplications, is a form of *dhikr* that cleanses the soul. The Prophet Muhammad would say, "O Lord of the heavens and the earth and Lord of the Throne. Lord of all that there is and will be. I seek refuge in You from everything that You are empowered against. You are the First and the Last. There is nothing after You, as there was nothing before You. You are manifest. You are the Lord of all that appears and all that is concealed."[20] This is a form of *dhikr*. The key to understanding the prophets of God and their legacy is to study their supplications and *dhikr*. *Dhikr* is what distinguishes a person who walks the path of God.

There are those who look at the affairs of this world and feel unfulfilled by the material and the physical. They are convinced

---

20 Muslim (6551), al-Tirmidhi (3481 and 3400), Abu Dawud (5033), and Ibn Majah (3873 and 3831).

that there must be more, either before the beginning of time, during their time, or after their time. This is logical because our consciousness is a simple flicker in the vast span of time. Our consciousness is like an insect that flies for a short period before disappearing. Our consciousness is so limited. But it is still such a gift for it is an opportunity to absorb so much. To be dissatisfied with that moment of consciousness is the call of God within us. The call of God is that sense of restlessness and unsettlement. Having walked the path of life, with its love stories, hate stories, disappointments, aspirations, and betrayals, you look beyond all of that to the essence of truth. This is precisely what *dhikr* rekindles in the heart. There would be a great power within us if we responded to insecurity, boredom, fear, exuberance, and exaggeration by rekindling the remembrance of God. This is because we often exaggerate in demeaning ourselves in moments of disappointment and loss. We also exaggerate ourselves in moments of happiness and joy.

God reminds us that God sent the Qur'an to bring people from darkness into light (Q 2:257; 5:16; 14:1, 5; 33:43; 57:9; 65:11). This demands our attention. I will speak shortly about how this particularly applies to Muslims, but the Qur'an addresses humanity at large. Invoking the same theme, we are often reminded that God sent the Qur'an as a guide to address our hearts and intellects. It does not require that our intellect and heart be at war, nor that our soul be at odds with our intellectual ability. That guide is a light. It is the light of certitude. How many times does the Qur'an remind us that God is the path of light, the Light upon light (Q 24:35; 33:43; 57:9)? The nature of darkness is to retract when light is present. If light is present, darkness withdraws. Light overcomes darkness. The key, though, is whether you keep that light within you.

The inner light of so many Muslims has worn itself out and dwindled to the point of being extinguished. But they do not realize it. They could spend a lifetime not realizing that their light has gone out. The only way to search for the light is to look in a mirror. No one can tell you whether the light is still within you. Only God knows. I often hear people say, "My life is covered by folds of sin or darkness," but it is not true. Darkness will not cover light. If there is light, it will cut through the darkness. It will appear. It may be that you need a stronger and brighter light. You need the light to overcome you. But darkness, by its nature, is weaker than light.

It is *dhikr*. In *dhikr*, we remember the God who blew into us the breath of life (Q 38:72), decided our existence, and intended that existence as a gift. The Giver can have an intent. How we receive that gift, however, is a different matter entirely. The intent of the Giver remains the same whether the recipient accepts or rejects it, celebrates or hates it. But it was intended as a gift with a promise from God, "If you take and accept this gift as a gift, I will grow within you, and you will grow within Me." You are then on your way to becoming a Godly human being who can peel away the various layers that alienate you from your Maker, your only Maker, and from the intention of the Maker who willed that you exist in the first place.

Hubris often leads us to philosophize why we exist in a certain period, place, ethnic or social group, and not another. It is all hubris. The only true knowledge of our place within God's intentionality comes from God. Many younger people say, "I am not sure why I was created. I am not sure what my purpose is." It is not that older people know why they were created. Most older people simply grow tired of wondering and never obtaining an answer, so they stop asking. But that type of knowledge, certitude, and sense of peace with yourself and your place in history comes only from the One who formed the intentionality in the first place. That is your Maker. It comes only from a close and intimate friendship with your Maker. So many people speak with a sense of outrage, injury, and offense. "I do not have answers for why I am here, what I am doing, why I was born the way I was born," et cetera. If you are not in the habit of listening to God, however, do not complain that you do not have Godly answers.

There is a huge difference between listening to family, friends, tradition, or mosque, and listening to God. The latter comes only through *dhikr*. There are so many *hadith*s on the merits on *dhikr*; it is even described as superior to acts of charity or *jihad*.[21] The five daily prayers are not a gymnastic exercise. It is not about communion with the energies on the face of the earth. It is not about the rules of prayer. It is, as our scholars of old said, like knocking on the door of the Lord and saying, "I am once again here in Your presence."

One of my teachers once met Anwar Sadat, the former president of Egypt. He said, "They made an appointment for me six months prior to my meeting with Sadat. They told me precisely where I am going to meet him, and from what time to what time. They went over the protocol and the etiquette from the beginning till the end of the meeting. They told me what questions may be asked and what cannot be asked. They told me what topics can be broached and what topics cannot be broached." I have never forgotten this. Years later, he repeated it in one of his sermons and then smiled, saying, "I never appreciated how humble it is for God to receive us five times a day until I met with Sadat. Whenever I wish to knock on the Lord's door I only need to say, "*Allahu Akbar*," and I have

---

21 For a sampling of the *hadith* reports on the blessings, benefits, and superiority of *dhikr*, see al-Tirmidhi (3375, 3376 and 3377), Bukhari (6407), and Muslim (2695).

the Lord's attention. And I keep the Lord's attention for as long as I want. The Lord never turns me away. If I want it for two minutes, I get two minutes. If I want it for ten hours, I get ten hours."

You cannot separate faith from the reality of what faith is meant to bring into your life. Remember that it is a fundamental tenet of Islam that God is self-sufficient and immutable. God gains nothing from our practice. The gift of light, which is the gift of the Divine because the Divine is the light of the heavens and the earth, is to partake in Divinity. It is to see the Divine within. No amount of law, instruction, or dogma can make you find the light within unless you look deeply at a mirror. The objective of faith is to not only find the light, but to fully embrace it until it chases away the corners of darkness within us. The more we reach out to God, the Light upon light, the more God re-energizes and empowers that light within us. The more we reach out to false gods, and there are so many false gods, including nations, tribes, and organizations, that light eventually quivers and dims until it becomes so small that it requires a tremendous amount of effort to reignite it. As Muslims experience so many tragedies and injustices, the wise person would seek to be filled with as much of the light of our Maker as possible. The unwise person would say, "There is so much darkness around. I may as well let the light go out within me as well." Then all is lost. God says:

> *God is the Protector of those who believe. He brings*
> *them out of the darkness into the light. As for those who*
> *disbelieve, their protectors are the idols (taghut), bringing*
> *them out of the light into the darkness. (SQ 2:257)*

God makes a solemn promise that if you seek the path of light, God will hold your hand and take you out of darkness and into the light. But the second part of this verse has always made me pause. It has often been on my mind as I studied the history of humanity, the rise and fall of societies, the nature of tyranny, exploitation, racism, ethnocentrism, sexism, and the ways that human beings dominate and exploit others. When God's light shines within, your senses and desires long for the Beloved. You long, and you understand. True understanding descends upon you so that you see everything for what it is. Your heart is emptied of greed, jealousy, competition, pettiness, and hate. As the Qur'an describes it:

> *The servants of the Compassionate are those who*
> *walk softly on the earth, and when the ignorant*
> *address them, say, "Peace." (Q 25:63)*

People have not reflected upon why the verse says to tread "softly" on the earth. This is because your heart is so full of the Divine that the earth hardly feels your impact upon it. You do not stomp on the earth demanding that it submits to you. You and the earth submit to God.

Let us turn to the ethics of those who are full of God's light. The very nature of that light is that it rejects what the Qur'an calls *taghut. Taghut* is an old word of Aramaic and Syriac origin that refers to forms of injustice and inequity. Remember that the Qur'an reminds us that no religion is without a measure of light. God reminds us that Moses and Jesus were sent with books that had light in them (Q 5:44, 68). Yet the truth and test of light is that it draws you to beauty. It draws you to what is beautiful, just, merciful, and compassionate. If you claim to have light within but are blind to injustice and oppression, I suggest you have not acquired God's

Divine guidance. Rather, you have acquired a type of dependency, like a drug addiction, that gives you comfort at the expense of others. God's Divine guidance makes you averse to everything ungodly. It makes you averse to everything that is demonic or satanic. It makes you averse to everything represented by the images of suffering, powerlessness, oppression, harm, and tyranny.

I will give you one example. The *National Geographic* recently released an article about the excavations by Israeli authorities under the al-Aqsa Mosque.[22] The article notes that it only requires a minor accident for large parts of the mosque to crumble. The article also notes that the excavations would not be possible without confiscating and tearing down Palestinian homes that have belonged to certain families for centuries. After Israel confiscates and destroys the homes, Jewish settlers are often allowed to move in if the land will not be used for future excavations.

What immediately caught my attention was the literature on Israeli religious archaeology in the region. I was struck by what various commentators, especially Jewish and Christian theologians whom I respect, say about Israel's role in Jerusalem. Time and again, people I respect intellectually fail the test of light. Why? It is because they talk about all kinds of ethical issues relating to God and God's justice but fail to notice the suffering of Palestinians. It is as if Palestinians do not exist. They are so embedded in their imperial project that, with a straight face, they can talk about God's kingdom and the place of Israel in God's plan, and yet never notice the plight of the displaced and the refugees—those who are the direct victims of injustice and

---

22 See Andrew Lawler, "Maze of Tunnels Reveal Remains of Ancient Jerusalem," *National Geographic* (14 November 2019). The article later reappeared as the cover issue of the December 2019 edition of *National Geographic* magazine.

aggressive theological ideas in the West. Those who know the state of the Muslim world know that the level of Western hegemony has reached such a point that an Egyptian who raises a Palestinian flag in a soccer game will be arrested and charged, as happened recently. This Egyptian is currently in prison and will likely face a criminal sentence. You can raise a Palestinian flag anywhere in the United States and you will not be charged and sentenced. But that is the level of hegemony that the West has over the Muslim world today.

You cannot have God's light if you do not notice the suffering of those who suffer. There are those who claim to have the light and yet fail to notice the suffering of African Americans and what it means to be an African American in inner city Philadelphia, New York, Houston, or Dallas. Or what it means to be an African in Africa today, with governments that exist to serve the interests of the World Bank, France, or the Netherlands, while crushing millions of dark-skinned people every year, without conscience. You cannot claim to have God's light and be indifferent to the great inequities of our world today, especially our support for despotism and mass human rights violations. So long as these violations are committed against dark-skinned people, we let it pass. If committed against people that look like us, however, we are suddenly troubled. That hypocrisy is a sure sign that the Divine light is not within us. God reminds us time and again that God does not love the unjust and God does not accept injustice. Injustice and oppression are antithetical to the soul of Islam and the nature of Divine light.

That is precisely why, when you are drawn to light, you are drawn to beauty in all its forms. And beauty has the air of justice and equity. You do not think solely of your comfort or whether your needs are met. You are ignited by light to think of the suffering of others. It is like saying, "What is within me is that I exist to serve you." That is Islam. That has been Islam from the very beginning until today. Pray with me that Muslims remember that.

29 November 2019

5

Parables of Light and Darkness

I often pray to God the most basic and quintessential prayer that
opens the secrets of the heavens and the earth: "God, Light of
the heavens and the earth, bless me with light." If one ever wonders,
"Why be a Muslim? What is the truth of being a Muslim?" The
answer is that a Muslim is someone who walks the path of light to
attain light, to live in light, to die in light, and to be resurrected in
light. So much of the Qur'an warns us of the darkness within us
and the darkness that we are capable of creating. Darkness is not an
abstract philosophical category. It has physical manifestations that
surround us. When we see poverty, suffering, cruelty, and the lack of
empathy, mercy, and compassion, therein is darkness. When we see
hate instead of love, therein is darkness. We do not need to understand darkness philosophically. We experience it. We encounter it.
In this *khutbah*, we will walk with the Qur'an to see how it portrays
the difference between the path of light and the path of darkness.

It is they who have purchased error at the price of guidance.
Their commerce has not brought them profit, and they are
not rightly guided. Their parable is that of one who kindled
a fire, and when it lit up what was around him, God
took away their light, and left them in darkness, unseeing.
Deaf, dumb, and blind, they return not. (SQ 2:16-18)

This is one of the most powerful parables in the Qur'an that calls us to ourselves. The Arabic is endlessly fascinating. How does one purchase error at the price of guidance? At a most basic level, it means we ignore guidance and insist upon an erroneous path. However, the language of the verse tells you more. It talks specifically of those who begin with an aspiration toward guidance but who then get distracted and confused. In other words, they start on the path of faith but then deviate. For this reason, the Qur'an says, "Their parable is that of one who kindled a fire, and when it lit up what was around him, God took away their light and left them in darkness, unseeing" (SQ 2:17). God does not take away anyone's light unless they are responsible for it. As I said, the verse speaks of an aspiration for guidance. There is even perhaps an intuitive desire for light. How is it, then, that the light of the fire results in blindness? How, instead of leading to guidance, does the light of the fire avail a person nothing?

Human beings forget that true light is inner light. True guidance comes only from your relationship and intimacy with God. God tells us that God is closer to us than ourselves, but we do not know (Q 50:16). The fire that we light could be the fire of religious rhetoric. It could be the fire of material wealth. It could be the fire of law, public adoration, or prestige. Whatever it is, it started with the right intention. Yet it remains a physical phenomenon. True insight comes only from the touch of the Divine.

God continues to address the situation of those who fail to build an intimate relationship with God. Despite alighting a fire that was supposed to grant them the blessing of light, they live in darkness. In fact, they are as if "deaf, dumb, and blind" (SQ 2:18). This is because they relied upon their physical senses to reach the truth, and these physical senses led them nowhere.

Or a cloudburst from the sky, in which there is darkness,
thunder, and lightning. They put their fingers in their ears
against the thunderclaps, fearing death. And God encompasses
the disbelievers. The lightning all but snatches away their
sight. Whenever it shines for them, they walk therein, and
when darkness comes over them, they halt. Had God willed,
He would have taken away their hearing and their sight.
Truly God is Powerful over all things. (SQ 2:19-21)

Human beings exist in a perpetual state of anxiety, a state of endless questions. Questions about the future, fate, meaning, love, and mercy. Human beings are constantly bedazzled and puzzled. If you think of these things without bringing God into the equation, you are precisely like those tossed into a thunderstorm. There are scary things in that thunderstorm. Thunder is a symbol for every trial, tribulation, and disaster in life. You lose a loved one. You get divorced. You get sick. You lose a job. You fail in some form or another. The reaction of those without God is to be gripped by constant anxiety and to do something that is entirely meaningless, that is, to ignore the threat by putting their fingers in their ears. This will not protect them. It simply means the cycle of loss will be repeated.

God then gives us a remarkable hint. No one is left without the blessing of the possibility of light, which is represented by the lightning. When there is lightning, you start to walk: when you lose a loved one, for example, you may feel closer to God; when you lose a job, you may read more of the Qur'an; when in divorce proceedings, you may start to pray or concentrate in prayer. Alas, however, if you do not develop your inner light, you will take a few steps but soon enough the darkness will return. When you are no longer in mourning, fear, or anxiety, the sense of closeness to God withers away and you return to the same old patterns and habits. Darkness sets in again. God tells us that this will happen unless God grants you the inner light that enables you to see not through the senses, the ears, nose, or eyes, but through the heart.

Why be a Muslim? It is because Muslims are the people of light. A true Muslim shines light. That light manifests itself in everything that is characteristic of the Divine. It manifests itself in beauty, kindness, mercy, compassion, justice, and equity. God is Most Friendly and Loving (al-Wadud). If a Muslim does not manifest the Divine attributes of mercy, compassion, kindness, love, and empathy, they are precisely like those who lit the fire but still exist in darkness. They are exactly like those who go back and forth like a yo-yo. So many of us are like that. Something bad happens, and we feel closer to God. Something good happens, and we drift away again. This is just like the person who needs lightning to walk. As soon as the lightning is gone, they are in darkness once again.

I cannot underscore this enough. So many Muslims have forgotten this basic and simple truth. You cannot claim to be a Muslim unless that inner light shines from you and people look at you and say, "We see the attributes of the Divine through that person." I do not care what your qualifications are. I do not care how many times you pray. You cannot claim to be a Muslim if your existence does not leave an imprint on the world, like a DNA fingerprint of mercy, kindness, beauty, justice, and equity. If you are a Muslim who tolerates injustice and suffering, you are exactly like those in the parable. You lit the fire, but you are lost.

In Surah al-Nur, God presents us with a powerful narrative. God reminds us that we must develop an intimate relationship with God if we truly wish to be Muslim.

> *As for those who disbelieve, their deeds are like a mirage*
> *upon a desert plain which a thirsty man supposes is*
> *water, till when he comes upon it, he does not find it to*
> *be anything, but finds God there. He will then pay him*
> *his reckoning in full, and God is swift in reckoning.*
> *Or like the darkness of a fathomless sea, covered by*
> *waves with waves above them and clouds above them—*
> *darknesses, one above the other. When one puts out one's*
> *hand, one can hardly see it. He for whom God has not*
> *appointed any light has no light. (SQ 24:39-40)*

Think about this parable. We live our lives oblivious to the fact that we will die, and that the only truth that remains after our death is God. Whether we believe it or not, it does not change the reality. It is as if God tells us, "You can believe what you want, argue all you want, doubt all you want, be fussy all you want, be distracted all you want, philosophize all you want, go around pretending that you have careers, lives, families, and wealth all you want, but it is all like a mirage in the desert. It has no inner truth to it." When all is said and done, God will be there. God will receive you. Whether you believe it or not, God will be there.

Upon death, angels will receive you. These angels will appear demonic if you are cursed or blessed if you are saved. You may not want to think about it, but it is coming. You can do all you want to distract yourself, but it is coming. Those who ignore this truth exist within layers of false perception. These layers of false perception are the waves and the clouds referred to in this parable. You see the darkness of the clouds and may be apprehensive or fearful. You may take measures to protect yourself. What lies beyond the clouds is the atmosphere and another layer of darkness. In this confusing and layered path, you reach a point in which you doubt even your own reality. So, you hold out your hands and you cannot even see them.

Do you want to know what this means? Look at people when they say, "I do not know why I was born and what life means. I do not know if I should care about my neighbor or if we should be kind. I do not know if justice is a virtue or if beauty is a value." That is the person who puts out their hand and cannot even see it. If you want a more practical example, look at what is happening in the land of the Prophet, the Hijaz, with people dancing around like monkeys to music that has nothing to do with beauty or Islam.[23] You put out your hand and you cannot even see it. You may have a career. You may have friends. You may have family. But you will reach a point in life in which you say, "Oh my God, I am dying. The time has come." When that time comes, the delivery of truth is upon you.

When we speak of Islam, we mean that the only exit from this turbulent and endless cycle is to be touched by God's Hand so that light grows within and you are no longer troubled by darkness, anxiety, and distraction. Light grows within until your heart is not

---

23 An allusion to plans that were announced in June 2019 to open the first "*halal*" nightclub in Jeddah, Saudi Arabia, as part of a raft of new social policies introduced under the auspices of Muhammad Bin Salman.

in the material world, but with God. Light grows within as God teaches you the attributes of Divinity. You no longer question the value of justice, empathy, kindness, or mercy.

That is the path of a Muslim. If I could, I would go around the entire Muslim world to teach people their basic and fundamental relationship with light. We Muslims are the first people who have forgotten our relationship with the Qur'an. We have forgotten how the Qur'an chooses to raise us and condition our behavior and understanding. Seek the light, not the mirage. Do not light the fire and then become blind, because you became distracted, resentful, despairing, or angry. The fire itself could be a deception because you thought that light would come from the fire, not God.

8 November 2019

PART II

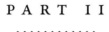

*On Love
and
Building a
Relationship
with God*

6

Your Existence Is No Coincidence

All the prophets of God taught the moral lesson of meaning. This is a huge part of our faith. By "meaning," I mean that we are not the result of mere coincidence or accident. From the moment of creation, there is an intentionality for our existence. Each of us exists because of a Divine intent for us to exist. We are not the product of happenstance. Human beings often forget the monumental importance of this. For if we exist by mere coincidence or accident, it is not a stretch to start believing that some of us are worth more than others, or that some of us have a greater right to exist or to more happiness than others. By its very logic, if coincidence is the teacher of morality and ethics, it also makes some rich and others poor. Those born wealthy through coincidence easily assume that luck has favored them. Because luck has favored them, they grant more value to themselves than to others. From this, we end up with the kind of imbalances seen all around. The population of a country like Britain can exploit and consume the populations of many countries around the world just so that the British can thrive. The population of a country like France can dominate, consume, and even destroy the population of Africa just so that those privileged by race, ethnicity, or nationality can thrive at the expense of those who are forgotten by history.

Study and reflect upon the prophets of God. The key lesson is that there is no coincidence and no accident. Everything created has a Creator. This logic is suspended only when we talk of the first cause of things. The logic of causality does not exist with the first cause but is a result of the first cause. Even those who do not believe in God ultimately throw up their hands at the first cause. They believe that at some point, somewhere, somehow, things like methane gas, carbon dioxide, and the raw material for stars came to be. When you ask them, "How did it come to be?" there is no answer. They say, "It just did." But when you give them the same logic about God, "Well, God just is and we do not know where God came from," they say, "No, we cannot accept that." It is a severe logical flaw.

Nevertheless, if God exists, then there is a reason for the creation of human beings. This is what all the prophets from Abraham to Muhammad have taught. That reason is not necessarily a justification. It may be that only God knows why a particular individual was created. But one cannot deny that God chose for every human being on the face of the earth to exist, Muslim and non-Muslim. Not only this, but God also created for every human being an entire bureaucracy or institution for accountability. For every person, there is a *qarin* or *jinn*-type creature that is the negative face of positive energy (Q 37:51; 43:36; 50:23). For every person, there are angels meticulously recording their deeds (Q 82:10-12). You are never alone. In addition, God is always present with you (Q 50:16; 57:4). Every human being on the face of this earth is so important. That is why God tells us that if you kill one human being, it is as if you have killed all of humanity, and that if you save one human being, it is as if you have saved all of humanity (Q 5:32). It defies the logic and order of Divinity to destroy God's creation, even if one human being. You negate Divinity by murdering one human being. You affirm Divinity by saving one human being.

The lessons of the Divine and the prophets do not stop there. Think of every prophet. Think of what secretive and powerful element allowed that prophet to build a community that educated the world. If I asked you to define that element, you may say, "Every prophet had faith." Faith can exist individually, but it is not what created the communities that enabled the prophets to leave their mark on the world. That secret and powerful element for every prophet, time and again, whether called "brotherhood" or "sisterhood" in some texts, is, in its nature and truth, love.

Witness the number of stories showing the intensity of love between Abraham and his disciples, family, wives, and children. Witness the number of narratives, whether in the Qur'an or the Old Testament, that talk of the love between Moses and his brother, Aaron, and the people of Israel. Read the stories of the love that Jesus had for his students and disciples and his passionate desire to see his people reform their ways out of love, care, and passion. See the bond of love between the Prophet and his people, whether *Muhajirun* (emigrants), *Ansar* (supporters), or, later, the Meccans whom he forgave and embraced so lovingly even though they spent a lifetime fighting him. This is why the Prophet reminds us in a report that those blessed with luminosity and purity on the Final Day will be "those who love one another (*al-mutahabbun*)."[24] This

---

24 Al-Tirmidhi (2390). See also al-Nawawi's (d. 676/1277) *Riyad al-Salihin* (381).

is not because they are attracted to one another's personality. It is not because they find it advantageous to like one another, or that circumstances created a family bond between them. Rather, it is because they love one another for the sake of God. Modern Muslims often think this means loving a person according to some formula found in the *Sunna* or *hadith*. No. It means understanding the worth of a human being as God's creature. It means understanding that every human being on the face of the earth has a reason and a purpose, and that if you respect God, you will respect God's creation. If you love God, you will love God's creation.

All the prophets of God came to tell people, "Do not waste your life worshipping mythologies. Do not let those who pretend to know the Divine Will exploit you, demand sacrifices, and suck your blood. Do not accept the mythology that some of you are a low caste and others are a high caste. Do not believe that some of you exist because God made them a chosen people, and that others are not chosen." Go back and read the stories of the prophets. Read them in relation to one another. You will find the message is always the same: you are here because God chose for you to be here. You are here because God has a purpose and an intentionality. Whether you understand this purpose and intentionality or not, you are worth so much that even the heavens take record of you. The heavens follow everything you do, day by day, minute by minute. They do this for every human being. When you kill a human being, you commit an offense against the heavens. It is as if you have exercised your own will over and above God's intent and objective when God said, "This human being shall exist." You do the same when you act like certain human beings are worth more than others.

Why is it, then, that we live in a world in which millions can be exterminated in a genocide in Rwanda and the world only slowly reacts? When millions were exterminated in a genocide in Congo, the world took forever to reach the Lusaka Agreement to stop the bloodshed.[25] It is because it is Africa. Why is it that NATO took affirmative action in Kosovo but the world only half-heartedly reacts to an ongoing genocide in Yemen? It is because Kosovo is in Europe and the victims were White. There is an ongoing genocide in Libya and the world contributes to the chaos, turning it into an opportunity to sell weapons and get rich. Why is it that when Eastern Europe overthrew despotism and sought to build democratic states, White nations, meaning Europe, the U.S., and Canada, helped Eastern Europe democratize and to this day continue to help? When dark-skinned people aspire to build democracies, however, the world looks to profit before anything else. If democracy does not yield profits, the Western world does not help any dark-skinned country build a democracy. In the Muslim world in particular, the West has thrown all types of obstacles in its path. The way we support Khalifa Haftar in Libya is proof enough. Haftar is a completely American invention. He is a Libyan military general on whose behalf the CIA intervened when he was captured in Chad. He lived in the United States at the expense of our intelligence agencies for twenty years. Then, when it was time to overthrow the democratically elected government of Libya, we unleashed Haftar. The U.S., France, United Arab Emirates (UAE), Egypt, and Saudi Arabia all support Haftar.

The very reason and purpose of Islam is to rebel. The purpose of the prophecies of Abraham, Moses, and Jesus was to rebel against the classism, racism, elitism, and unfair institutions of human society. If as a Muslim you do not understand this, then you are as far

---

25 The Lusaka Ceasefire Agreement, signed 10 July 1999, was an attempt to end the Second Congo War. It was signed by the heads of state of Rwanda, Namibia, Angola, the Democratic Republic of Congo, Uganda, and Zimbabwe.

removed from Islam as is possible. Your relation to Islam is tenuous at best. Faith is not just about prayer or fasting. It is what is in the heart. Do you look at the world and at every human being and say, "*Mashallah*, I know you exist because God decided for you to exist. As someone who loves God, I love you. I love you simply because I love God"? That is the meaning of "those who love one another."

One of the most heartbreaking things about modern Muslims is that this understanding of the worth of the created in light of the Creator was once intuitive. I look at the ethics of earlier scholars in the context of their historical moment. I judge them by the standards of their age. When I look at their epistemological framework, I find that they cared. They cared because they understood that they lived in something that belonged to God and must be honored by God, for God. So, they cared about animals. They cared about trees, rivers, and mountains. Read *al-'Iqd al-Farid* ("The Unique Necklace") and see how much of its poetry is about valuing nature, loving animals, and loving human beings.[26] Yet, modern Muslims seem to think that Islam is primarily about ritual and that ritual is an objective in and of itself. Modern Muslims seem to think that you can claim to love God but be neutral about God's creation or indifferent as to who suffers, who lives, and who dies.

This translates in a concrete way for me in the field of human rights. I have said it before and will say it again: the reason I care so much about human rights is because I am Muslim. I say this to all the human rights activists that I meet. They look at me and smile, as if I am saying something to sound smart. I do not blame them. They are not accustomed to hearing this from Muslims. Just because a wrong belief, system, or practice has become widespread, however,

---

26 A classic of Arabic literature compiled in several volumes by the Andalusian scholar and poet, Ibn 'Abd Rabbih (d. 328/940).

does not and will never make it right. This basic theological premise is the heart and core of Islam. The Islam of the Prophet Muhammad is to love everything through God, by God, and for God.

A longtime family friend, who comes from a practicing Muslim family that has been in the United States for a long time, recently told me something that has affected me deeply. One of their children met a missionary group that convinced the child to convert to Christianity. The missionary group did not sell Christian theology as a pristine idea to believe in. Rather, it sold Christianity through a heavy dose of Islamophobia. In other words, they said, "Look at how horrible Islam is. Since it is so horrible, come to Jesus who loves you." The Islamophobia is not what hurts the most. It is that the child converted to Christianity because they found in the missionaries a group that gave them hugs and love. In Islamic centers, meanwhile, they found only coldness and a lack of passion and warmth. They found the *imam* was more concerned about lowering his gaze than listening to or caring for their feelings. They found the *imam* would not even look at a woman while talking to her. They found people insisting that women should be limited to a designated space rather than praying alongside men as their equals. They found it was a huge deal whether a woman could even speak in an Islamic center or not. They felt, while praying, the eyes of ten women on her to check whether her *hijab* was correct. The parents of the child say, "The reason our daughter became Christian is not because of anything particular to Christian theology. It is because her experience of Islamic centers was alienating to an intelligent, smart, and respectable American Muslim woman." To be more specific, they meant Islamic centers in southern California.

Let me be clear. I respect a person's belief, whether it is Islam or another faith. But what hurts is the way we fail our youth. I do not think we can convince our youth that we truly understand the value of human dignity if we do not at the same time treat our youth with dignity. This does not come from pretending to respect them. They are smart. They will know whether you respect them or not. They pick up on whether you think you are higher than them or whether you treat them as an equal. Yet, every *imam* acts as if they are God's gift on earth. They always look down from on high. Most *imams* will not even shake hands with a woman. We failed this girl as we have failed so many others. We chase away the most educated and accomplished in our communities. We do not attract them. Our message is, "You are smart. You are educated. You are talented. So, we do not want you." What do we expect? But what are we going to tell God? I am sure it has not even occurred to the *imam* of the place where this girl was raised that God will come to him and say, "You are responsible for the various ways you alienated this girl." But that is the truth.

We do not teach that Islam means to love one another for God and through God. This is not fake love. It is the love that comes from giving every human being their worth and dignity. And we have an expression in the modern world to describe the worth and dignity of human beings: human rights. You cannot pretend to be a good Muslim in this day and age if you do not respect human rights. If human rights are not core to your theology and faith, there is no hope.

I will give you one final example, which relates to the death of Muhammed Morsi.[27] The issue is not Morsi himself but the violation of the human rights of this individual until he died in an Egyptian prison. The United Nations Special Rapporteur, Agnès Callamard,

27 Muhammad Morsi served as Egypt's first democratically elected President between 30 June 2012 to 3 July 2013. Morsi died in an Egyptian prison on 17 June 2019.

recently issued a report about the murder of Morsi through negligence and intent.[28] It kills me that all the discussion on the importance of a human rights report like this comes from non-Muslims. *Amnesty International* recently released another report on extensive human rights violations in Egypt. It included the plight of a woman, Aisha al-Shater, who has a rare disease that causes her to constantly bleed. *Amnesty International* is calling upon the world to pay attention to the plight of this poor woman in an Egyptian prison who is on the verge of a torturous death. Yet again, the only people who care about what happens to Aisha al-Shater are non-Muslims.

The UAE supports Haftar amid the murder of children and civilians in Libya. The International Criminal Court (ICC) has indicted one of Haftar's officers, Mahmud al-Werfalli, but Haftar has refused to surrender him. The UAE plays a critical role in modern day slavery by capturing and selling people. Along with Saudi Arabia, it also sponsors slaughter in Yemen. Yet Hamza Yusuf has delivered a public lecture in which he praised the UAE for its alleged "great leadership" of the Muslim world and for teaching "Muslim tolerance."[29] He is praising the UAE despite the slaughter in Yemen and Libya! Let us not even start discussing the Uyghur Muslims and how we have failed them. Three million Uyghur men, women, and children are suffering daily, and Muslims are absent.

You cannot claim to be a good Muslim if you do not care about human rights. In modern epistemology, caring for human rights is a short-hand way of saying, "I respect the dignity and worth of every

---

28 As of December 2021, Callamard is the ex-U.N. Special Rapporteur on extrajudicial, summary, or arbitrary executions.

29 On Hamza Yusuf's close ties to the UAE and silence in the face of despotism, injustice, and human rights violations, see The Usuli Institute, *The Last Ten Days of Ramadan and Bearing Witness for Shaytan* (*Khutbah*, 30 April 2021), and *The Price of Silence, Nicki Minaj, and the U.S. Human Rights Commission* (*Khutbah*, 12 July 2019). See also other references to Hamza Yusuf in this volume.

human being. I do so because I respect God's creation and I love God. So, I love God's creation." This is the faith. This is what Islam is about. Even if a day comes in which I am the only one articulating this message, I know it to be the truth. This is what all these books have taught me through an entire life spent reading and studying the Islamic tradition.

22 November 2019

7

On Love and a Loving God in Islam

I t is so easy to lose oneself in distraction in a shrunken world of mass information, mass communication, and technology. It is easy to lose sight of the fact that we belong to a faith with the creed that what comes from God must be beautiful, and anything that is not beautiful cannot come from our Lord. Our Lord, by definition, is the source of light. Light means beauty and purity. The idea that ugliness can coexist with Divinity is a contradiction in terms. It is impossible.

In our day and age, we are not familiar with how Islam was described in the pre-modern age. We normally translate Islam, somewhat inaccurately, as "submission." But submission comes from the fact of recognition, and recognition comes from the imperative of love. In Islamic theology, the reason God created the heavens and the earth was not to obtain meaningless ritualistic acts of worship. God created the heavens and the earth, and particularly human beings as opposed to angels, to have the love that God has for humanity reciprocated. God's creation of humanity was a loving, creative act. For this reason, Adam was entrusted with the "names" and the angels were ordered to prostrate before him (Q 2:30-32). It is because Adam was an expression of God's act of love, a magnanimous, magnificent, powerful, overwhelming, and loving act of creation. God has loved God's creation from the very first moment. God continues to love creation until the Hereafter. Yet God expects human beings to recognize this love, and to truly recognize it is to love it back. Put simply, without recognition, there can be no love. If you simply project yourself onto something, instead of recognizing it, you only recognize yourself. You assume the self is the truth of the other. That is an act of self-idolatry. It is *shirk*. You must recognize God as God's true self. The "names" that God taught Adam are the attributes of how we can understand the truth of God.

Until the rise of the Wahhabi-Salafi movement, it was taken for granted in Islamic theology that the act of creation was an act of love, and that God is a loving God. It was elementary. God was considered not simply a generous or indulgent God, but a loving God. God was seen as caring for human beings and loving them so much as to respect their autonomy and self-determination. If they acknowledge that love, they have its rewards. If they do not acknowledge that love—and they are free to do so—they drift away from the only true source of light and beauty in the heavens and the earth. The failure to recognize the Lord leaves you in the hands of whatever is the opposite of the Lord. This could be the whimsicalness, despotism, and unsettlement of the self. It could be the many ungodly and demonic forces in the universe.

Reading the pre-modern Islamic tradition often surprises me. Texts like *Kashf al-Asrar* ("The Unveiling of Mysteries")[30] are what we would today call "Sufi" works. In reality, the designation "Sufi" is now used so carelessly. It is as if anyone who does not see Islam through the arid eyes of the modern age is a Sufi. Many thinkers in the pre-modern age wrote that the ultimate act of love by the Divine was creation itself. Every moment that God gives you, God does so regardless of who you are, whether disobedient or obedient. God sustains you whether you are a saint or a monster. Even those who deny God wake up and exist moment to moment. Their molecules assemble and do not disintegrate for they are held together by the power of God. Creation itself is held together by the power of God. Deniers enjoy the benefits of eyesight, taste, and hearing. They enjoy all the bounties of the Lord. God's act of love extends to even the most disobedient. God provides, and continues to provide, every single instant until the moment of expiration. At that moment, it is as if God says, "I am sorry, but your time is up. Every moment of every day, I gave you an opportunity to recognize the love that I extended to you throughout your life. Now you must come back to Me."

This is because of the imperative of beauty. Justice is a precondition of beauty; if there is no justice, there can be no beauty. It would be unjust if those who did good were treated exactly like those who did bad. If it is unjust, it is ugly. That is why the very logic of beauty dictates the very logic of accountability. God can forgive. God is the

---

30 Qur'anic commentary by Rashid al-Din Maybudi (d. 519-20/1126), a twelfth-century scholar from Maybud, near Yazd in central Iran. The largest Sunni commentary in the Persian language, the full title of the work is *Kashf al-Asrar wa-'Uddat al-Abrar* ("The Unveiling of Mysteries and Provisions of the Righteous").

Most Loving, the Most Merciful, and the Most Compassionate. In an act of magnanimity, God can forgive anyone for anything. But God's forgiveness operates within the logic of sustaining the principle of beauty that has, at its very core, the principle of justice. If God forgave all sinners for everything they had ever done, treating them equally with those who reciprocated God's love, we would innately recognize it as unfair, ugly, and lacking in beauty. If it is lacking beauty, it cannot be from the Lord.

Every moment of every day, God renews that commitment of love that began with Adam. God is closer to you than your jugular vein (Q 50:16). God is there the minute you call upon God, even if one minute ago you were disobeying God in every way. For so long as you breathe, it is never too late. You can access the Lord by an act of supplication. The Prophet described prayers as acts of supplication to the Lord. In essence, that is what prayers are. You may have never prayed in your life, but the moment you start to pray, God is there to accept it with open arms and a welcoming heart. God reminds us in Surah al-Nur of the basic truth that those who have not been given light by the Lord have no light (Q 24:40). The only source of true beautification and light is the Lord. Everything else is a delusion.

Particularly in the age of modernity, we imagine loves and desires. We imagine grievances, hurt, and pain. We bear grudges. We have narratives of unhappiness and victimhood, sorrow and self-pity. Despite everything that modernity offers, at our core we remain unsatisfied. We remain uprooted and restless. For our only true anchor is the light that comes from our Lord. Everything else is a mirage. God describes it in Surah al-Nur as a mirage that you approach because you think therein is water. Once you reach it, however, you find there is no water. There is no good, save your Lord (Q 24:39).

I am always struck by the repeated language of love in our theological texts up until the 1930s. It is not an exaggeration to say that for earlier Muslim thinkers, it was elementary that creation was founded on love. We find this even in the works of Ibn Taymiyya (d. 728/1328), Ibn Qayyim al-Jawziyya (d. 751/1350), and other famous theologians. We of course see it in the works of Ibn 'Arabi (d. 638/1240), Hafiz (d. 793/1390), and Rumi (d. 672/1273). The core description of our Lord was that of a loving God. That is why God continues to forgive, guide, and give us a fresh start until the very last breath of our life.

We have somehow turned away from this. In the modern age, Muslims often cite the *hadith* that says that if the earth meant anything to God, God would not have given even a drink of water to an unbeliever.[31] But modern Muslims do not even understand this *hadith*. They also ignore the commentaries that emerged from *hadith*s like this. It does not mean that God does not love the earth, and therefore allows unbelievers to enjoy bounties. Rather, it means that the earth and everything that is in it is nothing compared to the mercy, compassion, and benevolence of God. Modern Muslims may have never heard all the *hadith*s on love as the purpose of creation. It is amazing. I believe our fortunes may start changing as Muslims if we make our hearts tender with the recognition that the greatest act of worship is not blind obedience. Rather, it is to reciprocate God's love.

In Surah al-Nur, God describes those who drift from the love of God:

> *Or like the darkness of a fathomless sea, covered*
> *by waves with waves above them and clouds above*

---

31 Al-Tirmidhi (2320).

them—darknesses, one above the other. When one puts
out one's hand, one can hardly see it. He for whom God
has not appointed any light has no light. (SQ 24:40)

God says elsewhere:

And if you drift away from God, God will replace you with
the people that God loves, and they love God. (Q 5:54)

God's love precedes the love of human beings. God's love comes first, and human beings reciprocate that love. If we do not understand the value of what it means to acknowledge God's love, we cannot reciprocate it. For we do not even recognize it. If we do not reciprocate it, we exist in folds of darkness because love is light, light is beauty, and beauty is the Lord. How could it be more elementary and basic than this?

Islam is not the religion of submission or obedience. Islam is the religion of love. It is shocking to see that Christianity, the religion that in the pre-modern age was associated with witch hunts and inquisitions, has stolen the language of love from Muslims and now posits and constructs itself as the religion of love. Meanwhile, Islam, which for centuries was the religion of a loving God, has become the religion of austerity, severity, and harshness. Is this why God lets us suffer the consequences of our idiocies and frivolities in the modern age? Wherever you turn, you find Muslims suffering. Is it because for several centuries we have forgotten our loving Lord, and have instead fallen in love with laws, rules, and dictates, until we found ourselves drifting in the waves of darkness that Surah al-Nur talks about? Is it because we have become the religion of attire, superficiality, pietistic affectation, and false appearance? Is it because we have become the religion of beards, *hijab*s, and *miswak*s (teeth cleaning twigs)? Where is that theology of love that for centuries inspired creative acts of beauty in art, painting, architecture, and music? Such passion only comes from love. Is it because we have mummified our religion to the point that it has become a dried-up edifice? Is it because of the despotism of rulers that co-opt religion and present it only from the perspective that serves power? Rulers do not like religions that teach love if they cannot control it. People in love do things that are unpredictable and uncontrollable. Rulers prefer religions that teach people obedience because that is easier to control. Is it because of the authoritarianism and despotism that have reigned in Muslim lands for the past centuries?

I do not know. But I do know that the truth of Islam must be reclaimed. We must return to the texts of the theologians that founded the interpretive tradition of Islam. We must return to the very concept of *tawhid* (monotheism). *Tawhid* is not about obedience. *Tawhid* is about love. It comes from love, and it returns to love. If you obey your Lord but do not love your Lord, you will never truly know your Lord. You will only know the law. There is only one way to access your Lord, and that is through love. If your heart does not skip a beat when you pray, your prayer is simply a physical act. This is something that you must strive for and work toward.

Dark sea, dark waves, and dark clouds (Q 24:40). It so often feels like this in our day and age. You either extend your hands to try to see your own self, or you recognize that there is only one Savior, the source of all light. The former is to be self-referential. It is when your only question in darkness is to panic, and ask, "Where am I? Can I see my hand?" Or you extend your hand for the Lord to take it. These are the two responses to darkness.

One of the subjects that I teach is human trafficking. I was recently reading some dark material about the organ trade in the modern age. There are several books exploring the two million Muslims currently held in concentration camps in China. Every Muslim in these camps has had their blood type and biological information recorded so that the Chinese government can turn them into an organ donor at a moment's notice. These books, none of which are written by Muslims, talk about how the Chinese government shoots Muslims in the chest or stomach and brings in a doctor as they lay dying to take their kidneys and liver, without anesthesia, to then trade on the black market. China trades in approximately one hundred thousand human organs per year. Most of these organs come from concentration camps that detain Muslims. The hardest part to read were the testimonials of Chinese defectors that said a large portion of these organs are sold to Saudi Arabia.[32] I then recalled what the so-called "Guardian of the Two Holy Shrines," Muhammad Bin Salman, said about these concentration camps, namely, that China has a right to defend itself from "terrorism."[33] What type of darkness allows human beings to harvest the organs of others? What type of darkness makes the entire Muslim world silent as two million Muslims perish in concentration camps? What type of darkness allows for the blessings of modern science to be used for a cause as demonic as organ harvesting? What type of darkness allows for a country that is, in principle, meant to represent the sanctity of Islam to become the largest consumer of trafficked organs of Muslims in China? For American Muslims, what type of darkness allows the U.S. government to not even attempt to hold China accountable for its genocide against Muslims?

---

32 For more on the trafficking of Muslim organs as part of the global 'halal' organ trade, see The Usuli Institute, *Trafficking 'Halal' Organs and Other Symbolic Signs of Our State* (*Khutbah*, 22 October 2021).

33 See footnote 12.

Those whom God has not given light have no light (Q 24:40). It does not matter if you build the highest and fanciest of buildings. It does not matter if you pray at the Ka'ba night and day. If you do not understand the meaning of God's love, you do not understand light. If you do not understand light, you do not understand beauty. If you understood beauty, you would rather die than buy the organ harvested from a human being in a concentration camp. You would understand that God will curse you and your progeny if you save the life of your child by purchasing a kidney stolen from another child in a concentration camp. You would understand the meaning of Islam. And this is the meaning of Islam: it is a God of love who loves beauty, not these dark ugly acts.

Until Muslims wake up and what you hear today is heard in every *jumu'a* around the Muslim world, until Muslims come to represent ethics, beauty, and love, God will leave us like those drifting in dark seas to the point that we cannot even see our own hands. May God bring these dark days to an end.

12 April 2019

8

The Prophet's Prayer of Love

The Prophet would often repeat the *du'a'*, "God, grant me Your love, the love of those who love You, and the love of every deed that brings me closer to Your love."[34] Like so many others, if we internalized and truly reflected upon this *du'a'* of the Prophet, it would transform our lives. To covet the love of your Lord, to see it as the ultimate objective, and to share and exist in that love; the entire trajectory of your being becomes all about that love. If you love something, it is your objective. If your objective is the love of God, you love only what is beloved by God.

You know what type of deeds, principles, and morals are within you. You know what brings you closer to God as an object worthy of God's love, and what does not. Moreover, there is a huge gulf between those who exist in the intoxication of the love of God and those who simply desire to squeeze by, whose ultimate hope is to do just enough to avoid punishment or to earn reward. There is a huge

---

34 Al-Timirdhi (3235, 3490, and 3491).

difference between those who say, "My goal is nothing less than to exist in a loving relationship with God," and those who say, "My goal is simply to perform enough deeds to avoid punishment or to be ultimately rewarded." The biggest difference is what shapes your heart, psychology, and state of consciousness. What moves you? What brings you to tears? What fills the gaps in your time? How do you understand your existence and your ultimate demise?

There is something else about those who persist in the *du'a'* of love. It is the very way they think of what is good and bad, and the way they assess the meaning of their lives. It is no longer acceptable for them to feel nothing or little, or to simply perform ritual obligations. Rather, there is a passion, a sweetness, a type of perfume of existence that they long for and covet. They search for the fulfillment of that longing in every act that defines their relationship with God.

Most Muslims may have read or encountered this *du'a'* at some point. Yet our Prophet would not pass a single prayer without repeating it. If that does not underscore the centrality of a *du'a'* like this in our lives, it is difficult to imagine what would. I believe this is the difference between those for whom Islam is a moral universe, the very foundation of meaning in their life, and those who deal with Islam as an inherited identity, who simply take Islam as a package with everything else they inherited from their parents. Like their genetic makeup, Islam is simply what they know, not what they truly desire and love. There is a huge difference between living with what you have inherited and living with what you have a passion for. When you say, "God, grant me Your Love," this does not simply mean, "Forgive my sins," "Grant me heaven," or "Grant me Your pleasure." It goes well beyond that. You are in effect saying, "God, grant me a passion for You. Grant me a fluttering of the heart, a skip of a beat. Grant me that inner call that makes me unsatisfied with anything unless it enables my passion for You." It reaches the point that you come to see even your career, school, and relationships in terms of whether they fulfill that longing and passion for God, or whether they simply sustain you and allow you to perform whatever you hope grants you salvation in the end.

There is another big difference. When you pray for love and persist in the prayer for love, God answers your call. God tells us that God is closer to us than our jugular vein (Q 50:16). When you feel that love, you acknowledge in the depths of your soul that God is present. Those who do not make the *du'a'* of love nor seek the path of love will often never feel the presence of their Lord. They see God, perhaps, like a watcher. When they think of God, they think God sees them like a spy camera, observing their actions. At most, they may think, "I should not sin because God sees me." But they do not feel the intoxication and elevation of the presence of the Lord. That is entirely different. It is when you do not simply think of God as a watcher, but you feel God as a companion.

The love of God is already there, ready to receive whoever accepts it and wants it. It is present. It precedes. It is the primordial state. God's love sustains the heavens and the earth. It is the Higgs boson that holds creation together. Without it, matter would cease to be matter. Trees would evaporate. Mountains would become like woven wool, puffed up and dissipated, as the Qur'an describes (Q 101:5). Birds would no longer be suspended in the sky (Q 16:79). Creation itself would be folded up like a book (Q 21:104). The Higgs boson holds everything together. The Higgs boson of existence is God's love. It is what allows matter to be matter. Your prayer is to acknowledge and reciprocate that love, and you cannot have what you do not pray for.

As infants and children, we grow from a state of utter dependency in the womb of our mothers. We are plagued with a gripping narcissism. We want shelter. We want nourishment. We want care and love. The challenge as we grow up is to shed that narcissism. Enlightenment is to realize that our freedom ends when the freedoms of others begin. In other words, it is to learn the balance (*mizan*) of existence, that is, that we human beings balance each other, and that all of us have equal rights, souls, and dignities. That is the challenge of growth. Those who remain with Satan never shed their narcissism. Existence begins and ends with them. They never develop healthy attachments to society or to others. Yet lovers in the path of God want something beyond that. They want that innate sense of passion that, when they were born, they may have directed at their mothers. They now want to direct it at the true Mother of existence, as if to say, "We have migrated from the narcissism of infancy to the enlightenment of knowing that all along, from the get-go, You were at the beginning and the end."

Lord, we know that because of our longing for love, we have done many things that were ill-advised, misdirected, and outright disastrous. Because of our longing for love, we started out by loving ourselves. Because of our longing for love, we first thought that our parents were the center of existence. Because of our longing for love, we have loved the wrong woman or man. Because of our hunger and thirst for love, we have done many things that were not right. We may have even violated the rules guiding how we should honor Your loan to us, our bodies, by engaging in sexual relations outside of marriage. The ultimate act of maturity, however, if you complete your migration to God, is to realize, "Lord, from the very beginning it was You, and only You. From the time we were born, when we cried for our mothers, we were really crying for You. We may have attended a party and broke Your laws by doing things we should not have done, but we were really longing for You. When we went out with someone or did inappropriate things, we were really longing for You." That is the path of love. You realize that it was always, from the beginning, longing for God and for nothing but God.

God's love sustains and holds you even as you think of all the ways that human beings defile God's gift of love. God granted us this wondrous earth and gave us a simple charge: do not corrupt the earth (Q 2:11; 7:56). We corrupt the earth by destroying God's creation. The least you can do as a human being is not destroy the gift. That is why God accuses those who arrogantly treat the earth as they please—destroying, killing, plundering, and amassing wealth—as acting as if they are as tall as mountains (Q 17:37). That is the Qur'anic metaphor. It means your ego is out of control. It is an act of *taghut*, meaning oppression and despotism.

You raise your hands, praying to God for that passion of love, and then the earth interferes. The affairs of this world invade your space as you learn that in the city in which the Prophet was born, Mecca, the holiest of holies, another thirty-seven people have been executed. Among them was a child. For most, their crime was that they were Shi'a Muslims who dared to raise their voice to demand a more just existence. You turn to look another way, and in Sri Lanka some Muslims have blown themselves up and killed hundreds of people. In Yemen, the slaughter continues. In Libya, colonial powers support a CIA agent to rule the country and impose another military dictatorship.[35] In Syria, the slaughter continues unbounded. In Egypt, another Pharaoh plants himself on the throne and tells people, "I am

---

35 The "CIA agent" alluded to here is Khalifa Haftar. For more on Haftar, see Chapter 6: *Your Existence is No Coincidence* in this volume.

your god, obey me."[36] The dream is that, at a minimum, all Muslims have a right that the land of the Prophet honors us, represents us, and embodies the values of God's love; that it does not represent the pillaging, plundering, despotism, and injustice of the demonic on this earth. We Muslims have that right, regardless of what colonial powers, imperialism, or arrogant and myopic nationalism say. We have a right to be honored by the cities of the Prophet, his family, and his Companions. We also have that right in our Jerusalem.

Turn to God and say, "God, this is Your earth. This is Your land. This is Your creation. I do not know what I, as a human being, can do, but allow me, God, to not be distracted by the suffering and injustice, and to feel the sweetness, elevation, and perfume of Your love, so that I am not deceived into thinking that You have given up on existence." If you are a seeker in the path of love, then at that very moment you will feel God's presence consoling you, telling you, "What you see as a lifetime, I see as but a nanosecond in existence. What you see as a story of tragedy and suffering, I see as a future of promises. Those who are with Me, I am with them. Those who do not know that to love Me is to establish justice can pillage, plunder, commit injustice and murder, and believe that somehow that brings them closer to Me." Those who seek the path of love know better. They know it is impossible for God's love to be approached through murder, mayhem, injustice, despotism, and suffering. It is impossible.

Pray for God's love. Pray that God grants you the sweetness of love. Pray that you feel that passion. Pray that you feel God's presence that surrounds you and embraces you all the time, at every moment.

26 April 2019

---

36 An allusion to Egyptian ruler 'Abdul Fattah al-Sisi and the self-deification of the Qur'anic Pharaoh (Q 79:24).

9

The Lifeline of Prayer, Perseverance, and Patience

O ur earmark is that we are people of the Qur'an. This is the essence of who we are. It is the pulse that animates us and the energy that motivates us. This is so for everyone who attends a *jumu'a* and who self-identifies as Muslim. When 'Aisha, the wife of the Prophet, was asked, "How was the Prophet during his lifetime?" her response was simple: "His character was the Qur'an."[37] Worldly affairs offer trial and tribulation, challenge, distraction, and digression, but what hearkens us back to the essence of our soul, to the very fiber of our being, is the Qur'an.

If you want to understand the health of the Muslim *Ummah* at any time in history, examine its relationship with the Qur'an. When the *Ummah* is healthy, you find Muslims engage the Qur'an on so many levels. You find all kinds of studies, commentaries, and

---

37 Muslim (746).

explanations of the Qur'an. You find the Qur'an is the essence of their being. When the Muslim *Ummah* is unhealthy, you find their relationship to the Qur'an is tenuous and unstable. I will give you a simple example. Compare the number of Qur'anic studies and commentaries written between the pre-modern and modern periods. Compare not only their volume, but their depth and sophistication. Modern Muslims, for all their technology, rhetoric, and dogma, have produced very little in terms of study, reflection, and interpretation of the Qur'an. They often approach the Qur'an as if searching for ammunition for the battles of their day and age, rather than as an ethical core that directs their very being.

All Muslims feel challenged. Reflecting upon our day and age, there is so much that challenges our understanding and sense of dignity. From the massacres of the Rohingyas to the plight of Muslims in China, which continues with so little attention from the rest of the Muslim world. From the plight of Muslims in Syria and Iraq to the obscenity of what is happening in Yemen. I could go on. Most shocking is Jerusalem, a place once described as the "bride of Islam," and the lack of passion among contemporary Muslims as to what is happening there. When I feel my heart constrained and heavy with all that exists in our world, I find there is nothing to turn to, no salvation or guide, other than the Qur'an.

There is so much that constantly speaks to you when you turn to the Qur'an. It is as if the words of God echo in your very being.

Persevere in prayer at the edges of the day
and parts of the night. (Q 11:114)

Scholars disagree as to whether the "edges of the day" refers to morning and *Zuhr* prayers or to *Zuhr* and *Maghrib* (evening) prayers. In any case, the meaning of the verse is that the day should be defined by your prayers.

Truly good deeds remove those that are evil . . . (SQ 11:114)

The law of your Lord is that goodness will in due time erase evil. This is the law of nature and creation. You have no recourse other than to turn to your Lord in sincere prayer. Muslims may excel in electronics today. They may spend monumental amounts of time on the internet. But a true relationship with God comes from persevering in prayer. It comes from knowing how to truly pray and how to spend the night in prayers.

In Surah al-Muzzammil, God teaches that the soul and intellect learn to be in balance in the night (Q 73:6). You uphold that dynamic as much as you invest in your prayers and inner reflection upon your relationship with God. You allow goodness to persevere on earth, regardless of the challenges, deceptions, or how much it seems to have eluded people. For this reason, God tells us:

This is truly a reminder for the wise, the sagacious.
Persevere with patience: God does not waste
the results of good deeds. (Q 11:114-115)

Persevere with patience. The formula is to pray into the night so that you learn to balance yourself. This means not chasing after other human beings, finding fault in others, or spending time spewing out empty talk. It means choosing instead to spend hours alone with no one but God, even if it feels extremely uncomfortable. Not a computer, television, or entertainment. Nothing but you and God, your Maker, deep into the night.

In so doing, you elevate yourself as a human being. God leaves you with knowledge that perseverance and patience is the key. There is a formula; the winners are the perseverant and patient, not the restless and despairing. I say this because we cannot kid ourselves. So many of us today have become despairing and restless. We want Islam, but we do not know how to build a relationship with God and the Qur'an is not the heart of our being. We do not spend hours reflecting upon the revelation of the Lord. Even if we memorize the Qur'an and even if we pray, we do not know the sweetness of faith and the way it softens the heart and shines a light within that exudes outward. Once nestled in your heart, the sweetness of faith gives you that formula. It is the goodness that erases the bad. This becomes the essence of your being. You become incapable of doing anything but what is kind, merciful, and compassionate. It is as if once you truly establish prayer, the switch in human beings that enables them to be hurtful, dishonest, and deceitful is turned off. Those with true prayer in their heart have nothing but goodness (*hasanat*).

I wish modern Muslims would reflect upon that one expression: *hasanat*. Goodness is universal. All human beings smile. All respond to kindness and love. All respond to compassion and joy. We do not need sophisticated dogma and philosophy to understand the nature of goodness that should flow from our relationship with the Most Compassionate, Most Merciful. How can someone claim to have a relationship with the Most Compassionate and Most Merciful and not be compassionate and merciful themselves? There is something broken there. If you want to test the state of your faith, look at yourself through the eyes of those who know you. Do they know you as a loving, compassionate, and merciful human being? Do you reflect the ethics that come from your Lord?

Persevere because God does not waste good deeds. Persevere because God knows that to focus and concentrate in prayer is difficult. Persevere because God knows if and when you want to quickly finish your prayers and run off to the next thing. Persevere because God knows that this temporal world runs at an alarming rate that is not compatible with human psychology. Persevere because God knows that many around you will attempt to distract you from the path of your Lord. Persevere because God knows that there are periods in history of raging hardship and genocide in which the average Muslim is tested, and says, "Where is my Lord?" Persevere because God knows there will be many pretenders who claim to know the Lord, but who act in cruel and ugly ways. For all these reasons:

Persevere with patience. God does not waste
the results of good deeds. (Q 11:115)

Ultimately, in Surah Hud, the Qur'an ends with a proclamation and a reminder from God:

And thy Lord would never destroy the towns unjustly,
while their people were reforming. (SQ 11:117)

God does not allow people, cities, countries, and nations to deteriorate and be swept away other than by their own injustice. God's law of creation is that justice brings goodness and blessings, and injustice destroys a people. This is why we need patience and perseverance. We need to teach this to our children so that they do not despair and have doubts about the faith and their relationship with God. If you teach them the nature of patience and perseverance, and they see you as an example of this, you will affirm in them an unwavering belief in goodness and beauty. They will follow you. They will emulate you. They will do as you do. So, be an example to your children. Especially at this time, as Muslims in the West are tested by Islamophobia, hatred, and bigotry. Your children confront it every single day they go to school or college. They have nothing, and you have nothing, other than your relationship with the Lord.

1 February 2019

PART III

Keeping Our Faith in the Modern Day

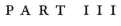

10

Thinking Islam Anew Away from the Lands of Despotism and Hypocrisy

We live in strange times. We live in times that call upon us to dig deep within ourselves to define our relationship to God and Islam, and to ask ourselves: what does Islam mean to us? What does Islam mean to the world? What is the message of *fitra*? When God describes Islam as the religion of *fitra* (Q 30:30), it should make us pause and reflect. As the religion of *fitra,* Islam should by its very logic appeal to thinking and ethical human beings. It should not appeal to immoral, unethical, and ugly human beings. If Islam, as we interpret and practice it, instinctively appeals to immoral and ugly human beings, then something is wrong. If Islam appeals to the most ethical, moral, just, and beautiful human beings, then something is right. Islam did not come to destroy the moral fabric of individuals. Islam did not come to say that what God created within the very consciousness, awareness, and understanding of human beings is flawed and must be re-engineered. Islam came to augment what is good and to resist what is bad. We often ignore what it means to say that Islam is the religion of *fitra*.

In this vein, I repeat, we live in odd times. But they are potentially liberating times. Many years ago, I wrote a book, titled *The Authoritative and Authoritarian.*[38] I had encountered Muslims of every type in the West and found that much of what they insisted upon was based on the most superficial knowledge of the *hadith* literature. Much of it was authoritarian because it imposed a despotic regime upon the intellects and hearts of human beings. Twenty years ago, for example, everywhere you turned, people insisted that music is *haram* (forbidden). Music, however, is encoded in our genetic make-up. It is as instinctive and intuitive to the fabric of human beings as language or a sense of happiness and sadness. Yet people would cite well-known authorities to say that this was a conclusive matter. They claimed there was *ijmaʿ* (consensus) on the matter. It was not open for debate or discussion. People would also say that pictures, photographs, and drawings are *haram*. They would say that befriending or seeking peaceful coexistence with non-Muslims is undesirable. The nature of a Muslim, they claimed, is to do precisely the opposite of what non-Muslims do. We were repeatedly told that it is the *Sunna* of the Prophet to adopt nothing of the culture, values, or practices of the West.

These assertions were so unequivocal, so uncompromising. We were also told that a woman's voice is part of her *ʿawra* (private parts that must be covered); that the mosque of a woman is her home; that she should obey her husband as if she is obeying God; and that the pleasure of God is contingent upon the pleasure of her husband. We

---

38 See Khaled Abou El Fadl, *The Authoritative and the Authoritarian in Islamic Discourses: A Contemporary Case Study,* 3rd edition (Al-Saadawi Publications, 2002); *And God Knows the Soldiers: The Authoritative and Authoritarian in Islamic Discourses* (Lanham, MD: University Press of America, 2001).

were told that interacting with the opposite sex is *haram* and that social activity outside of the home for women is *haram*. The list of *haram*s went on and on. I wrote *The Authoritative and Authoritarian* to challenge this type of unnatural Islam, an Islam that makes people feel awkward, uncomfortable, and lacking in inner peace. I faced attacks left and right. "You want to Westernize Islam." "You want to liberalize Islam." "You are progressive. You do not like Islam the way it is, so you want to change it." Repeatedly, I told people that the Islam they imagine is an artificial and invented Islam. It is an Islam fabricated in the modern age for reasons that have nothing to do with the intuitive, beautiful, and serene message of the Islamic faith.

The years go by, and we find ourselves living in these rather strange times. The same clerics who once called me a person of "innovation and heresy," who put me on blacklists, and who declared that I should not be allowed to speak at Islamic events, have, lo and behold, discovered overnight that music was not *haram* after all. Not only this, but they have come to some odd, even ironic, conclusions. These clerics now declare that Mariah Carey, with her exposed bosom, is an acceptable form of entertainment, yet they still insist that methods of reciting the Qur'an that observe the rules of tonality and music are *haram*. Apparently, the recitations of 'Abdul Basit and *Shaykh* Tablawi are *haram*, but Mariah Carey is not.[39] We live in odd times.

One of these clerics once declared that it was *haram* for women to watch soccer matches because they would see the exposed thighs of soccer players and could get aroused, which may cause problems with their husbands. This cleric now claims, overnight, without

---

39 An allusion to a Mariah Carey concert that took place in Jeddah, Saudi Arabia, on 31 January 2019. Carey performed in front of a mixed-gender audience. Her publicists are reported to have defended the concert, claiming that it was a "positive step toward the dissolution of gender segregation" in the country.

explanation, that it is *halal* (permitted) for women to not only attend soccer matches, but even hip-hop concerts. The same clerics that for years said it is *haram* for men and women to interact in mosques or at work now say that there is no problem with them attending music concerts. I, the so-called "liberal" and "progressive," would not attend these concerts because my Islamic sense of character would find it distasteful and morally uncomfortable. These same clerics have for years told us that it is *haram* to have pictures inside the home. Yet I recently saw an image of a group of children, aged five or six, standing in line next to a picture of the King of Saudi Arabia. As the children passed by the picture, they declared their allegiance to the picture of the King. If that does not remind you of idolatry, I do not know what will. These same clerics said for decades that playing chess is an unforgivable sin. Yet I recently saw a video of a prominent Wahhabi *Shaykh* playing cards in a new entertainment center, smiling broadly as he forgot all the misery that he had brought upon Muslims for the last thirty years.

These so-called scholars have trained generations of *imam*s to come to the U.S. to teach Islam. They have for decades called people like me "liberal," "progressive," and "Westernized." It does not take a genius to know why they changed overnight. They changed because the King or Crown Prince of Saudi Arabia wanted the change. It is as simple as that. No juristic explanations. No *fiqh*. No method or research. But it does not stop there.

These are the same clerics who have blessed and praised the destruction of the homes of 'Aisha, Abu Bakr, and 'Umar Ibn al-Khattab in Mecca. They have blessed the destruction of thousand-year-old mosques in Mecca. In their place, luxury hotel skyscrapers have been built. The Ka'ba was once the jewel and heart of Mecca, but today it appears small and shrunken amid the high rises. It gets even worse. There is currently a project to expand the *Haram* (holy site) in Mecca. It has been contracted to the *Saudi Binladin Group*,[40] which has subcontracted it to Western companies to further westernize and anglicize the architecture and city planning of Mecca. Mecca already looks like a place for rich people. If you are not rich, you feel alienated and foreign in Mecca. The rich can buy nice apartments with views of the Ka'ba, as if it is a tourist attraction. Instead of visiting and reading Surah al-Fatiha for Abu Bakr, you can now go to the luxury *Hilton Hotel* where the home of Abu Bakr used to stand. The new expansion will destroy whatever remains, and very little remains of the Islamic heritage of Mecca.

Show me a bigger *bid'a* (innovation) than this. Show me a greater lack of respect for methodology and Islamic history and tradition. We no longer have *fiqh* or *Shari'a* coming from that part of the world. We have an absolute mess brought about by despotism, oppression, and the desire to be in the good graces of an Islamophobe, Donald Trump. Is it not ironic that while Donald Trump builds a career by attacking Muslims and epitomizing Islamophobia, the *imam* of Mecca, 'Abdul Rahman al-Sudais, says, "With the blessings of Muhammad Bin Salman and Donald Trump, Saudi Arabia and the U.S are leading the world." He brags that he is in the hands of an Islamophobe, someone who has made clear his hatred for Muslims.

What is the point in saying all of this? The point is that God has blessed us because the masks of hypocrisy have fallen. God has reminded us that Islam is the religion of *fitra*, of instinct, intuition, reasonableness, and beauty. First, build your faith. Becoming pious is a preliminary step. Pray, fast, and build your Islamic sensibilities. Then, if someone tells you the voice of a woman is *'awra*, say, "Where you

---

40 A multinational construction conglomerate, based in Jeddah, known since 2019 as the *Binladin Group Global Holding Company*.

learned this doctrine is suspect. I will consult my Muslim intuition and ask if it is reasonable or beautiful." If someone says a picture is *haram* or that you must obey your husband blindly or that you must do this or be segregated there, all the garbage that we have lived through for thirty years, immediately say, "I consult the religion of *fitra*. Is it reasonable? Is it beautiful?" When God commands justice and beauty (Q 16:90), is God talking to us like we are animals who cannot be expected to comprehend? Or does God expect us to have a sense of what justice and beauty are? Consult yourself. Does this sound just? Does this sound beautiful? If it leads to my oppression, marginalization, or degradation, is it just? Is it beautiful? If your heart is uncomfortable because you suspect it is not just or beautiful, say, "Excuse me. I am not a scholar and I do not know the technicalities of whatever *hadith* you are citing, but until I have an opportunity to consult a scholar that I trust, a real scholar who shines beauty, piety, and serenity, not a scholar who changes overnight because his boss tells him to, or a scholar of harshness, intolerance, and fanaticism, you can keep your advice to yourself. Thank you very much, but I do not want to hear it."

This is the methodology. God has blessed us that the hypocrisy has exposed the hypocrites. This is a new chapter for Muslims, especially those in the West. To the Islam that comes from lands of despotism and hypocrisy, meaning Egyptian Islam, Saudi Islam, and Emirati Islam, say, "Thank you very much, but keep it to yourself. I will find a scholar who reaches my heart. I will consult with them about the evidence. In the meantime, I am doing what my sensibilities tell me is beautiful and just." This is a transformative moment because the hypocrisy, lies, and ugliness have become intolerable.

When I started my critique of puritanical Islam all those years ago, people asked me, "Why are you raising these issues?" I raised them because I foresaw that it would lead to the chaos of today, where things are turned on and off purely at the whims of a despot. There are those who think that true Islam will come from overseas. I think they are deluded. It has become abundantly clear that Muslims in the West must see themselves as the original pioneers of Islam, especially those who rediscover or convert to the faith and who know that this is a message of justice and beauty to humanity. Ask yourself what Islam, as a message of justice and beauty to humanity, should entail in this moment. What does justice and beauty as a gift to humanity mean? Liberate your thought from the garbage that comes from the colonized, dominated, and subjugated Middle East, and say, "I am a pioneer of Islam. As a pioneer of Islam, I must ask myself the question anew as if I am writing a new page. I must work on my piety and think about justice and beauty as a moral imperative for Muslims here and now."

In closing, I want to reflect upon something that I have been struggling with. We have all heard about the recent visit of the Pope to the United Arab Emirates.[41] We heard about the stadium that he filled and the prayer that he uttered. We have heard that he met the *Shaykh* of al-Azhar and of the tolerance initiatives that they launched. That is fine. Religious tolerance is justice and beauty. Who can say something negative about that? But there is something that still bothers my heart. The Pope visited a Muslim country that is complicit in a genocide in which thousands of Yemeni children have perished and Yemeni women have been trafficked into prostitution. I work in human trafficking, and I see the results. The Yemeni government has done nothing about the sexual assaults committed by Yemeni forces against Yemeni women. Meanwhile, prisons in Yemen and

---

41 On 3 February 2019, the head of the Catholic Church, Pope Francis, arrived in the United Arab Emirates for the first ever visit by a pontiff to the Arabian Peninsula.

the UAE are full of Muslim scholars who are tortured, humiliated, and murdered. This is just like the prisons of Saudi Arabia, Egypt, Algeria, and Syria.

The Pope visits the UAE and says a prayer for the people and children of Yemen. As Muslims, is this the point we have reached? Do we have no dignity? We are so happy that the Pope has come to a Muslim land, led prayer, and was kind enough to meet the *Shaykh* of al-Azhar. Where is the Islam in which Muslims do not have such an insecurity that needs to be fulfilled by others? Where is the Islam of Muslims who are not so insecure as to need the Pope to affirm, "You are okay." Muslims celebrated when the Pope said Islam is not a violent religion. It was as if his testament is all we need to feel good about our religion. We should instead be asking: "Your Holiness, Pope, sir, how about the genocide? How about the people in prison who are tortured and killed as you go around with leaders who are responsible for systematic human rights violations?"

"God commands justice and beauty" (Q 16:90). It is as simple as that. Is this just? Is this beautiful? Is genocide just and beautiful? Is it just and beautiful for the rich elite to praise each other while ignoring those who suffer? It is time for us to be the pioneers of Islam. It is time for us to say, "This is not Islam. None of this is Islam. We pray that God guides you and somehow heals your hearts." We must think anew as Muslims in the United States and the West. We must think on a blank page. Our Islamic faith must invite us to think as moral human beings about what is most just and most beautiful. Therein will be the straight path to the Lord.

15 February 2019

11

Recolonization, Racism, and the Role of Reason

There was a considerable response to the previous *khutbah*.[42] Every response, whether positive or negative, is an invitation to reflect. The nature of knowledge and the search for the Divine is to never rest with a lazy confidence in unchallenged certitudes. A Muslim is an intelligent human being. The nature of intelligence is to despise and reject indolence. It is to reject the comfort that leads to laziness. The nature of intelligence is to always be searching. For this reason, Ibn al-Mubarak (d. 181/797), an early jurist of Islam, claimed that a person remains worthy of being described as a scholar for so long as they seek knowledge; once they believe they have attained knowledge, they become an ignorant human being; they are no longer a scholar.[43] The nature of scholarship is to never rest

---

42 See Chapter 10: *Thinking Islam Anew Away from the Lands of Despotism and Hypocrisy* in this volume.
43 Ahmad b. Marwa al-Dinuri, *al-Mujalasa wa jawahir al-'ilm* (Beirut: Dar Ibn Hazm, 1419/1998) 2/186.

on one's laurels. It is to never assume that one knows. A student of knowledge will always find that they do not know far more than what they do. I mention this as a segue to a critical issue.

We live in a day and age in which Muslims around the world, especially in the Middle East, are recolonized through very clear processes of domination and subjugation. Muslims are recolonized politically, economically, militarily, and, most important of all, intellectually. Muslims are recolonized through a process of carefully negotiating who in power can act as a proxy to control the Muslim masses so that they do not challenge—and I pick my words very carefully—the racist paradigms of the global elite. The global elite is a racist elite. If not White in skin, it is White in culture. It is an elite that since the sixteenth century has dominated darker-skinned human beings through deeply racist paradigms. In the seventeenth century, there emerged the so-called science of forensic anthropology that, for the first time in history, divided human beings into races: Negroids, Caucasians, Mongoloids, and so on. This was a major step in human history for it was not simply a scientific venture. Rather, it was an attempt to define human beings racially so that the White race, the Caucasians, could create a monopoly over all the beautiful attributes of humanity, such as rationality, virtue, morality, and reason, and attribute all of what was demeaning and degrading to the non-White race, such as irrationalism, despotism, and so on.

This racial logic was thoroughly supported by legal institutions. Most people do not know that until as late as 1965, for example, Muslims could not become citizens of the U.S. Until 1954, race was still grounds for exclusion in the U.S. Until this very day, national quotas are a thinly disguised system of racism to maintain the racial purity of the U.S. and Europe. So, Muslims are colonized. When you see the invasion of Western corporatism into the heart of Mecca and Medina, you realize that Muslims are colonized. When you see American officials intervening in educational curricula in the Muslim world or deciding whether Muslims are worthy of democracy or human rights, you realize that Muslims are colonized.

There is a further type of colonization that is far more sinister in our day and age. It is the colonial enterprise of Islamophobia. This is deeply sinister for it is able to penetrate the hearts and minds of our Muslim youth, implanting in them so many seeds of doubt, until they are faced with a fundamental choice: they either attempt to use their intellect, but the Islamophobes have convinced them that if they do so, they will inevitably accept the conclusions of the Islamophobes, or they put their intellect aside and join the ranks of the dummies of Islam. By the "dummies of Islam," I mean those who do not live in our contemporary world in any real sense because they live by a literalist reading of classical texts and traditions, which they are untrained to read and cannot properly understand.

This creates enormous challenges. This very week, nine young men were executed in Egypt. There is no doubt that these men were tortured. Confessions were obtained. They had nothing to do with the crime for which they were convicted. The executions were unjust. Now, this would be yet another injustice in a Muslim land but for one very telling thing. According to Egyptian law, all death sentences must be sent to the institution responsible for issuing *fatwa*s in Egypt, *Dar al-Ifta' al-Misriyya*,[44] which then issues an advisory opinion as to whether the execution is in accord with the *Shari'a*. *Dar al-Ifta'* approved the execution of these nine men. Since this procedure was created by the British, it has never opposed a single

---

44 On *Dar al-Ifta'*, see footnote 13.

execution, including the execution of someone like Sayyid Qutb (d. 1386/1966).

But *Dar al-Ifta'* went a step further. It not only approved the executions. Shortly thereafter, in response to widespread anger, it engaged in Islamophobia. *Dar al-Ifta'* released an image of a bearded man, wearing traditional Arab garb, talking to someone wearing trousers and a shirt. The image said: "Beware of terrorists. Don't let them fool you." So, the beard and traditional dress have become an image for terrorism, while the shirt and trousers have become an image for reasonableness? If this is not evidence of complicity in Islamophobia, I do not know what is. *Dar al-Ifta'* not only spread this image. It also issued a false declaration, claiming that the men were members of the Muslim Brotherhood (MB) and that Egyptians must remain vigilant in fighting the MB because it is a terrorist organization. In so doing, *Dar al-Ifta'* was clearly implying that we should not care about the murder of these young men or their heartbroken mothers; we should not care whether their confessions were obtained through torture, or what human rights organizations are saying about the way they were convicted and killed; we should not care about any of this because we have an obligation to fight the MB and "political Islam." There is no evidence that the men belonged to the MB. But even if they did, does it matter?

Does this not indicate the colonization of the Muslim mind? Is this not evidence of the construction of Islamophobia within Muslim cultures? What is greater proof of the internalization of Islamophobia in our culture than the Crown Prince of Saudi Arabia, Muhammad Bin Salman (MBS), stomping on top of the Ka'ba?[45] MBS is so alienated from his tradition that he does not realize that,

---

45 A reference to the incident from 12 February 2019, when Muhammad Bin Salman was filmed walking on top of the Ka'ba with advisors.

as you approach the Ka'ba, you should be shaking from reverence. He has no reverence because he was raised as an Islamophobe. Why do I say all of this? It is because we have been reminded, once again, that religious institutions in dictatorial and despotic countries are marred in hypocrisy. Their credibility does not stand up to scrutiny. We, Muslims in the West, must not look to these institutions for authority or guidance. And we must be on alert that the hypocrisy of the "homelands" can easily be implanted into the hearts of those who come from these countries as figures of authority in the West. You do not leave your hypocrisy at the door just because you came to the U.S. Once a coward, always a coward. Once you learn to kiss up to rulers in Egypt, Saudi Arabia, or the UAE, the rot of hypocrisy is in your heart. Your faith becomes egotistical and narcissistic because you lose touch with God. To have God in the heart is to have the courage and power of defiance, even if the cost is everything. Once you learn to be a coward, however, your faith becomes an exercise in egoism, narcissism, and self-promotion. You become as if a parasite that feeds off the disempowerment of others. This is because you have compromised your own sense of integrity, autonomy, and power.

There are specific steps. First, you must recognize something foul when it exists, and what is happening in countries like Egypt and Saudi Arabia is foul to the core. This does not mean that you should exclude all those who come from these countries. What it means is that you must be wary of those who are anchored in this culture and who propose to teach you Islam. Second, know that no religion has honored the intellect more than Islam. We know from *hadith*s of the Prophet that God did not create anything more revered to God than reason (*al-'aql*). The Islamic tradition is replete with *hadith*s of the Prophet in which reason is described as the "pillar" of a believer (*da'amat al-mu'min*).[46] These *hadith*s remind Muslims that the intellect was not created to be put on the shelf while reading a text. The Prophet said that the Qur'an—even the Qur'an—will do no good if it is read irrationally or without applying the rigors of the intellect. Some Muslims think they can simply read a *hadith*, put their intellect and reason on the shelf, and—*voila!*—have their Islam. What do we expect from this, especially when those who read the *hadith* have the hypocrisy of despotism in their hearts? Converts always complain about how ugly things are. The ugliness comes from the hypocrisy of despotism. But you can create beauty when you liberate yourself and realize that God gave you the gift of reason. So, glorify and sanctify the gift of reason within you. It is not there to be denied. It is there to be nurtured and nourished.

Third, seek knowledge. Let us dip briefly into the ocean of traditions about the duty of seeking knowledge. Think of the *hadith*, which is no longer heard in the modern age, in which the Prophet says that the most secure people in the Hereafter are those who are most reflective.[47] In another *hadith*, the Prophet is reported to have said that while all human beings sin, those with developed rational faculties need not fear sinning; their rational faculties are such that their conscience awakens them and calls them back to reason.[48] In yet another *hadith*, the Prophet says that a single word of wisdom is dearer to God than the entire earth and what is in it.[49] We are a religion that essentially tells people to reflect, to use reason, to not simply be puppets moved by strings, and to reject living a life of subjugation to others. Be what God wants for you. Do not be the

46 Al-Ghazali, *Ihya'*, 1/308. Also Walid al-Zubayri, ed. *Mawsu'a al-Hafiz Ibn Hajar al-Asqalani al-Hadithiyya* (Leeds, UK: Al-Hikma, 1422/2002), 5/423.
47 Al-Ghazali, *Ihya'*, 1/282.
48 Muhammad Mahdi Naraqi, *Jami' al-Sa'adat* (Tehran: 1428/2007), 1/124.
49 Al-Ghazali, *Ihya'*, 1/142.

subservient, obedient, broken, dishonored, and undignified human beings that we see all over the world. That is not what God wants.

To restate: know what and who you should be suspicious of; glorify your reason; be vigilant in pursuing knowledge; and know that God has created people with different abilities and talents. Distrust those with a career in medicine or engineering who love to play the role of a Muslim jurist, or the jurist who loves to play the role of a medical doctor. Know that these people are pretenders and have ego issues. They are not at peace with themselves. Islam is too serious and too honorable to be treated as an extracurricular activity. In despotic countries, children do not specialize in the Islamic intellectual tradition because their parents fear it could lead to their disappearance in prison. For this reason, parents tell their children to become doctors, engineers, or computer scientists. As a result, in the West, our ideas about Islamic history, theology, and philosophy have come from those who are busy making a living and who teach Islam on the weekend. This is offensive to the core! With all due respect to all surgeons, medical doctors, businessmen, and stock traders, systems of knowledge in the modern age require specialization and dedication. Do your job and excel at your job. If you want to help Islam, support those who have dedicated their lives to the study of the Islamic tradition.

Seek those with a dedication to knowledge, but always ask yourself: "Is what they give me lifting them at my expense?" This is the litmus test for any *fatwa*. In legal terms, we call it a conflict of interest. "Does that *fatwa* give them something at my expense?" It could be something material, or something like power or authority. If so, you have reasons to be suspicious and you need to study the issue further. If not, then you can start to consider what they are saying. This is the starting point of a methodology for Muslims in the West to become the ray of hope for an entire Muslim *Ummah* that has been recolonized, re-subjugated, and re-dominated in the most grotesque and ugly way. We, Muslims in the West, have a heavy obligation upon our shoulders. We are called upon to lead the *Ummah*. Not in a military sense—that is nonsense. Leadership today is through information and ideas. Leaders today are those with a heavier bank account of ideas and who get to monopolize meaning and epistemology in the world. That is the power of the modern world. Those who define the terms, control the language. And those who control the language, control everything.

22 February 2019

12

Resisting the Colonization
of Muslim Minds

I do not surprise anyone in saying that these are challenging times for Muslims. Muslims all over the world are plagued by powerlessness. It is not that they do not have the means to power. Muslims, collectively, control over half of the world's natural energy resources. In terms of size, they number well over one billion. Muslims have at their fingertips everything that would enable them to be empowered in the modern world. Instead, Muslims continue to be disempowered in a variety of ways. One of the challenges of being disempowered is that Muslims are largely led by corrupt puppets who, while ruling Muslim countries, in fact rule for someone else's interests. Since the colonial era, it is common for a Muslim ruler to rule over Muslim lands but to answer to non-Muslims. The responsive constituency of the ruler is not their own people but rather the powers that have effectively colonized the territory over which they preside. For the President of Egypt, 'Abdul Fattah al-Sisi, for example, it is far more important what Europe or the U.S. thinks or wants, rather than the Egyptian people themselves. It is the same for Saudi Arabia, the United Arab Emirates, Jordan, and so many Muslim countries.

That is the epitome of disempowerment. It is when collectively, as a people, you do not matter. There is no means by which you can translate your desires, preferences, or willpower into a means for self-determination and autonomy. Whoever rules over you is not interested in being accountable to you as a people. They are interested in being accountable to those outside their supposed constituency.

Awareness is a key part of the equation. Every single human being must define their relationship with the ideas of autonomy and self-determination. At a most basic level, a person may think that if they can enjoy themselves or indulge in distractions, they are exercising autonomy and self-determination. But the falsity of this is obvious. You could have all the fun in the world but ultimately lack the power to control what happens to your home, family, or children. You could lack the power to in any way influence your spiritual, moral, or intellectual progress; you only have the power to entertain and distract yourself. This explains what is happening today in Saudi Arabia. The Saudi government is opening all forms of entertainment to give the Saudi people the illusion of autonomy and self-determination. In typical authoritarian format, the idea is that if you can party, you are autonomous. Meanwhile, the Saudi people control nothing about what happens at the national or multinational level. They are, in fact, entirely powerless and without self-determination.

Similarly, another form of delusion is to believe that if you can fight, you are autonomous. It is to convince people, particularly the young, that if they engage in violent acts and are killed in the process, they somehow control their destiny. In fact, they die in vain because their death causes only a minor discomfort for the rest of the world. This is another form of disempowerment.

The only true venue for self-determination in our day and age is the flow of information. The flow of information shapes, crafts, chisels, and defines consciousness. This is precisely why Islamophobia is such an extreme form of disempowerment. When you manage and manipulate information in such a way as to create a sense of dread among Muslims and non-Muslims about Islamic theology, law, and history, you have affected the autonomy and trajectory of Muslims in clear and undeniable ways. It is critical for Muslims to understand that what we call Islamophobia is a movement to control information to create deep-seated insecurities in the hearts and minds of Muslims about their own tradition. This has reached extreme levels that many Muslims are not even aware of.

You cannot say the word *"Shari'a"* anywhere in the Muslim world today, for example, without making Muslims uncomfortable. They are immediately gripped by a sense of dread. You must explain that you are not a fanatic. You are not a member of the Muslim Brotherhood. You are not an "Islamist" or a terrorist. Similarly, any Muslim who utters the word *"jihad"* immediately experiences a sense of dread, like a gulp in the throat. They immediately become suspect. They have to explain that they are not a bad person and do not mean anything evil by the word. In other words, they must engage in apologetics. Even when mentioning the words "Islam" or "Prophet Muhammad," Muslims feel a sense of dread. They must now explain that Islam is not violent, and that the Prophet was not bad. The minute you do that, you give up power. The minute you apologize for your being, your being has been compromised. Any human being placed constantly on the defensive loses self-determination.

Information is being controlled here to limit the ability of Muslims to engage in that magical discovery of the modern age: autonomy and self-determination. This is what I call the "colonization of the Muslim mind." To be clear, this does not mean injecting Western values into the Muslim mind because many Western values are simply the values of modernity. Rather, it means that you inject a sense of dread and insecurity into the Muslim mind about their own tradition, faith, and law. Take victims of abuse: the physical abuse, akin to the violent invasion of a country, is not in itself nearly as damaging as the psychological abuse, which tears apart the psychology of a human being through a great deal of insecurity, lack of confidence, and an impulsive need to apologize for oneself. This is precisely what has happened with modern Muslims.

People did not speak in terms of self-determination and autonomy before the industrial and scientific revolutions. This kind of language and the related ideas of free speech, human rights, or democracy are concepts that would have never occurred to pre-modern human beings. But autonomy and self-determination in the modern age are not the direct products of military power. Rather, they are the products of *informational* power. You could, in fact, be militarily quite humble but informationally and technologically have the ability to shape the consciousness and define the awareness of human beings. That gives you the power to define not only yourself, but others. *That* is self-determination and autonomy.

The idea of "no god but God" is an empowering idea. Monotheistic faith is a faith of empowerment. I have said before that all the prophets of God came to deliver the same message: worship God alone and realize your self-worth as a human being; you do not need a mediator with God; as a human being, no one may compromise the value of your life for it was given to you by God; the rich are not worth more than you; Whites are not worth more than you; the free are not worth more than you; all human beings are of equal worth because they are all creatures of God. That is the essence of monotheism.

Each prophet then comes in a repeated cycle to embrace the disempowered and to resist the powerful. This is the repeated cycle of the prophets. If monotheism leads to nothing but the practice of ritual, however, without elevating the sense of autonomy, independence, dignity, and self-confidence of the human being, then it is not working.

I often talk about the radical revolutionary idea of monotheistic faiths, that is, that there are no intermediaries with God; as a human being, you are so important as to deal with God directly. To say the least, Islamophobia succeeded in complicating this innate and self-evident value of *tawhid*. Tell Muslims today that the gift of Islam is to have a sense of dignity and self-worth that exceeds anything ever given to humanity. If they are honest with themselves, they will reply, "Really? Considering how things are today, can I really feel that sense of empowerment and euphoria?" The fact they cannot feel that sense of empowerment is precisely the disempowerment of Islamophobia. Muslims were colonized militarily and territorially and, for the most part, failed to resist. The problem is that the current form of colonialism—the colonialism of Islamophobia—is far more lethal and dangerous because most Muslims are not even aware that they are, in fact, colonized. Most are unaware that it is difficult for a Muslim's relationship to Islam to exist today without passing through the filter of Islamophobia.

There are some truly bizarre facts. In 2007, the *RAND Corporation* issued a report about the kind of Muslim that the West can live with.[50] Among other things, the report says that the West should fight terrorism by shaping the Muslim mind. It speaks very much like a colonial power, like how the French and Italians talked about shaping Algeria or Libyan identity. The report speaks of the type of "moderate Muslim" that the West must support, and lists as exemplars such figures as Ayaan Hirsi Ali and Irshad Manji. Hirsi Ali is an atheist, but she was still listed as an exemplar. Irshad Manji is effectively an atheist. Her connection with Islam is nonexistent. If you exist in a faith to hate everything in it, you are not embracing the faith; it is easy to camouflage as a critic. Some years after the report, Hirsi Ali gave a talk in Washington, DC, before an audience of politicians, diplomats, and other important figures.[51] To avoid war with Islam, she claimed, Islam must reform as per five conditions that she set out. One of the conditions is that Muslims must abandon the concept of *jihad*, denounce what she called "violence" in the Qur'an, no longer consider the Prophet Muhammad a moral exemplar, and so on. At the time, I thought Hirsi Ali was simply spewing out nonsense and that no one really cared what she was saying. I was completely wrong.

I was wrong because if you observe the type of Islam that is today promoted in the Muslim world in countries like Egypt, the UAE, Saudi Arabia, and on American-owned Arab TV stations like *Alhurra*, you find a group of figures who, in the name of "reforming Islam," promote an Islam that is indistinguishable from that of Hirsi Ali. I am referring to people like Ahmed 'Abdou Maher,

---

50 Angel Rabasa, Cheryl Bernard, Lowell H. Schwartz, and Peter Sickle. *Building Moderate Muslim Networks* (Santa Monica, CA: RAND Corporation, 2007).

51 A reference to a talk that Hirsi Ali gave to the National Press Club in Washington, DC on 7 April 2015. For more see Samuel Smith, "Ex-Muslim Ayaan Hirsi Ali Proposes 5 Changes To Islam That Could Help Lead Its Religious Reformation." *The Christian Post* (9 April 2015).

Khaled Montaser, Ibrahim Eissa, and Islam al-Behairy. These figures repeatedly talk about how Islam is a violent religion. Yet they talk as if they are good Muslims. They say, "We must discard most of the *Sunna* and abrogate the violent verses in the Qur'an." This is indistinguishable from what Islamophobes like Hirshi Ali say. I even know from private sources that when al-Azhar sought to respond to the accusations leveled against the Islamic tradition by 'Abdou Maher and al-Behairy, the Egyptian and UAE governments prevented them. Not only this, but when activists asked for equal access to present a counter-discourse, many of them were accused of belonging to the Muslim Brotherhood and arrested in the UAE, Saudi Arabia, and Egypt.

It gets even worse. One of the most amazing things has developed in the current Muslim world. We have not seen it since the vulgar days of early colonialism. I refer to the process by which Arab, Pakistani, Indian, Afghani, or Persian Christians pretend to be Muslim and seek to Christianize Islam from within. Let me give you one example. There is a Christian activist, John Mehr, who has hated Islam for decades. Mehr created an organization that he calls the "Muslim World Conscience for Human Rights." He prances around Europe speaking about the type of Islam that the West must "support," i.e., engineer and create. Among the members of this organization are Rachid Barbouch, a Moroccan, and Mustafa Rashid, an Egyptian. Rachid Barbouch claims to be the *mufti* (legal scholar) of Corsica. It transpires, of course, that Muslims in Corsica have never heard of him. It also turns out that he converted to Christianity decades ago and has since pretended to be a Muslim *imam*. As for Mustafa Rashid, it is not clear if he was born a Christian or is a convert to Christianity. Since 2006, however, he has pretended to be a Professor of *Shari'a* and an al-Azhar graduate. He is a constant presence on

Egyptian, Emirati, and Saudi media outlets. He cannot properly cite a single verse of the Qur'an and makes incredible mistakes about Islamic history, claiming, for example, that the Prophet was a Christian before becoming Muslim. According to Mustafa Rashid, Muslims do not have to fast, and alcohol and pork are allowed in Islam. You do not have to perform the *hajj* (pilgrimage to Mecca). According to Mustafa Rashid, there is no difference between the *tawhid* of Islam and the *tawhid* of Christianity. Why is he supported by media outlets in countries like Egypt and the UAE?[52]

This trajectory started in the West on a smaller scale shortly after the invasion of Iraq, which was the birth of the Islamophobia movement. At that time, many of those who played a critical role in the Islamophobia movement pretended to be native informants about Islam or converts from Islam. Think of someone like Mark Gabriel, for instance, who is extremely influential. Gabriel claimed to be trained as a *Shaykh* who taught at al-Azhar before converting to Christianity. He has written books attacking Islam in the U.S. It turns out, however, that Gabriel was never a Muslim and never a *Shaykh*. He, in fact, comes from a Coptic Christian family. Or consider Walid Shoebat, who is one of the most influential Islamophobes. Shoebat, a Palestinian, claimed to have been a terrorist before finding Jesus and converting to Christianity; Jesus, he claims, saved him from the evils of Islam. Yet, a CNN report investigated Shoebat and found that he was never a practicing Muslim or a terrorist.[53] He claims to have been arrested by Israeli authorities after attacking an Israeli

---

52 Each of these figures and organizations is widely discussed in Arab media sources.
53 See Drew Griffin and Kathleen Johnson, "'Ex-terrorist' rakes in homeland security bucks." *CNN* (14 July 2011). Note the following passage from the report: "But CNN reporters in the United States, Israel, and the Palestinian territories found no evidence that would support that biography. Neither Shoebat nor his business partner provided any proof of Shoebat's involvement in terrorism, despite repeated requests."

bank as a Muslim terrorist. According to the CNN report, the bank did not even exist, and he was never arrested.

What is most important is what you discover in the CNN report: Walid Shoebat makes around half a million dollars a year. He does this by giving training seminars on Islam to Homeland Security and the FBI. Look it up. This is what drives me crazy about Muslims: they are entirely clueless; they have zero idea that our federal government uses our tax money to hire someone like Walid Shoebat, a clear fraud, to teach that Islam is inherently violent, that every Muslim is inherently violent, and that there is no way to coexist with Muslims unless Muslims strip themselves naked and denounce even the Prophet Muhammad, just as Hirsi Ali says.

This process started in the West but has since been exported to Muslim countries. All over the Muslim world, you find voices who are supported by state media and who do nothing but disempower Muslims by creating a sense of dread in their hearts about their own tradition, the Prophet Muhammad, the Qur'an, and Islamic history. What are the concrete results of this? In the modern age, it is possible to affect the intellectual climate of the world. It is possible to affect the energy of ideas by ensuring that a certain idea takes over the world. What type of energy around Islam has taken over the world? It is the energy of dread. Any Muslim who does not admit to having some doubt toward their faith and the morality of the Prophet, Islamic history, and the Qur'an is lying. If this is not disempowerment, I do not know what is.

Remember that power is an attitude. If you have a strong sense of self-confidence, identity, and integrity, you are empowered. If you are broken, lowly, and humble, full of doubt and insecurity, you are disempowered. When you implant that attitude into the psyche of Muslims, you disempower them. You colonize them. It is time for

Muslims to wake up and realize that you do not have to occupy a country today to colonize it. You do not have to occupy territory to colonize it. You simply have to control information. I speak from personal experience: 99.9 percent of Muslim PhD students who study Islamic theology, philosophy, law, or history experience a crisis about their identity as a Muslim. "Can I actually be a good scholar and a good Muslim at the same time?" That tension does not exist objectively. It exists subjectively in the mind of the person. It exists because that person is victimized by the fact that Muslims do not control and influence the flow of information about Islamic history, law, philosophy, and theology.

I want to recommend a book, entitled *American Christians and Islam: Evangelical Culture and Muslims from the Colonial Period to the Age of Terrorism*.[54] The book shows how, since the colonial age, Christian evangelicals have sought to influence how Muslims relate to their own tradition. The book focuses on American evangelicalism, but the point can be applied to all Western missionary attitudes. Christian missionaries thought that if they cannot get Muslims to convert to Christianity, they can at least get Muslims to have a troubled relationship with their tradition: "If we cannot get them to be Christian, we can at least get them to be doubtful. For as long as they are doubtful and troubled, there is hope that someday they will convert to Christianity." American evangelism dedicated an enormous amount of resources to achieve that goal. Since the start of the War on Terror, American evangelism has awoken again to the dream of colonizing the Muslim mind. That is the story of Islamophobia. That is the story of our present reality.

---

54 Thomas S. Kidd, *American Christians and Islam: Evangelical Culture and Muslims from the Colonial Period to the Age of Terrorism* (Princeton, NJ: Princeton University Press, 2009).

The problem is that Muslims are in a state of slumber. The only way to resist this is by investing in knowledge, information, and data. The only way we can fight this fight is by realizing that our children, the future generations of Islam, will grow up with severe doubts about their faith. Many Muslim children all over the world are now atheists, agnostics, or converts to Christianity and we are not even honest about it. We cannot count on Muslim governments because these governments are colonized. We can only count on private resources.

This is the reality, and we cannot deny it. Our minds and the minds of our children and grandchildren have been colonized. Whether the active ingredient is evangelical Christianity, Catholic missionary Christianity, Zionist right-wing dogma, or just simple, good old-fashioned financial interests that want to control the decision-making processes when it comes to oil and money markets, it does not matter. The net effect is the same: the way you relate to your religion, tradition, and even your God has been penetrated, invaded, and colonized from within.

10 January 2020

13

Liberation from Mythology and the Power of a White Jesus

The message of the prophets of God has always been the same in its central themes, basic precepts, and normative ethics. It is a message that the prophets came to humanity to underscore time and again. It is summed up in that single phrase: "There is no god but God." Worship none but God and submit to none but God.

It is remarkable that God has repeatedly underscored this straightforward and simple message. From a historical perspective, this was always delivered in the context of two specific challenges. The first challenge is that human beings, throughout history, have been drawn to the idea of polytheism or *shirk*. Polytheism is the belief in multiple gods. It is sometimes a belief in the god of good and the god of evil; two gods that are in constant battle. Or it is a belief in the god of the sun and the god of darkness. Or the god of fire and the god of water, and so on. Anyone who reads ancient history is struck by the recurrence of the belief in one God and the constant shift toward polytheistic mythology. You can, in fact, read the history of religion as a constant tug of war between the two. You see this in Indian, Chinese, and Samarian mythology. You see it throughout Greek and Roman history. It is very pronounced in Egyptian mythology. Throughout the history of religion, there is a constant pull between the idea of the one and only God and a sociological dynamic that always mythologizes the one God into a pantheon of gods.

The belief in one God would have easily anchored itself in native cultures, without gravitating toward polytheism, had it lent itself to the demands of ancient power structures, and had it been consistent with the cultural and psychological orientations of ancient people. The modern mind tends to think of something as either temporal or Divine; something is either Divine or not Divine. But this is not how the ancient mind worked. The ancient mind saw Divinity as a gradation. One could start as a human being, for example, and become Divine. Or something could start Divine and become human. Animals could have a physical body but also be Divine in some sense. Elements, such as water or fire, could be observed, experienced, consumed, and yet somehow reflect Divinity.

This brings us to the second challenge. Why was the idea of monotheism so difficult to accept and so easily corrupted? Why is it that so many prophets encountered this, whether in the Qur'an, the Bible, or the Old Testament? The Old Testament is essentially a narrative of the trials and tribulations of a line of prophets who came to teach that there is only one God. We know from archaeology and history that even the Israelites, the people said to represent monotheism in ancient history, were always drawn to polytheism. Both before and after Moses, the Israelites adopted a virtual carnival of deities. Their monotheism was constantly corrupted.

Why, then, was monotheism so hard and polytheism so attractive to the ancient mind? One reason is that without the rational and casuistic methods of thinking, mythology was used to represent and symbolize meaning in the world. Beyond this, however, there was a serious pragmatic and political reason: the holders of wealth and political power in the ancient world always sought to lay claim to Divinity. Think of the ancient Hindu or Buddhist religions or the very concept of the kings or queens of old. They may be born human, but rare was the king or ruler who resisted the temptation of deification. For if the king is Divine, then disobeying or challenging the king becomes a crime that is unforgivable. In Roman and medieval common law, for instance, there was no separation between a crime against the state and a crime against majesty. This is the crime of *leges maiestatis* in Latin, meaning a crime against the emperor is also a crime against God, because the emperor is Divine. Think of how amazingly attractive this idea was to ancient power structures. If Divinity was strictly separated from temporality— meaning the Divine occupied its space and the temporal occupied its space—then kings, queens, priests, rabbis, and all types of holy men could not claim Divinity for themselves. If they could not claim Divinity for themselves, what would they do? They would have to relinquish privilege. Claiming Divinity was crucial to claiming and maintaining privilege.

Look at our world today and see how much of a hold this idea still has on the human mind. Look at dictatorial countries. Rulers are talked about in Saudi Arabia, the UAE, and Egypt as if they can literally commit no error and make no mistake. They are endlessly praised. Whatever they do is wonderful. Were they not Muslim, these rulers would surely have been deified. Had they existed in the ancient world, they would most certainly have become gods. It is a form of deification for all practical purposes.

God sends the same message that there is no god but God, but this message consistently clashes with the sociological reality of mythology, particularly a mythology that serves power structures. Rulers want to be deified. Noblemen want to be deified or semi-deified. Human beings want to claim a Divine-like right to be obeyed. To do that, there is always an alliance between the religious class and the ruling elite in which the religious class creates a mythology that serves the ruling elite. For this reason, God tells us that *shirk* is a great injustice (Q 31:13). God is not only talking about God's own Right. Rather, there is a practical and sociological consequence to the compromise of monotheism. It is that human beings deify other human beings or institutions. We know, for example, that for much of European history, the institution of the Church was deified. It could make no error and could, in fact, grant absolutions in God's stead. This gave the Church an enormous amount of power, which was leveraged for all types of causes and purposes. It also made the Church very rich.

It is critical that we understand the message of Islam against this historical backdrop. Monotheism has always posed a challenge to rulers and yet the tenacious hold of polytheistic mythology has continued even after Islam. You find mythologies of deification in 'Alawi or Ismaili groups and in some Sufi and Shi'a ideas that the barrier between the human and the Divine is not that solid. Because Islam has a strong monotheistic narrative, however, and because the Qur'an, unlike the Old and New Testaments, was historically preserved, the pull of polytheism has been camouflaged in highly sophisticated philosophies, like Ismaili theology, or in esoteric sects like Zaydi or 'Alawi theology. Or, it has been camouflaged in the doctrine of strict obedience to the ruler.

What does monotheism teach you? It first teaches that if you submit to God, you submit to no one else. Your liberation as a human being is through God because if you submit to God, you submit to no one lesser than God. That is a revolutionary idea. Throughout history, it has been a revolutionary idea. Submitting to no one but God means that no one can claim superiority over you, particularly the type of superiority that makes them feel entitled to obedience simply by status. Everyone must appeal to your reason or heart, not to mythology. Know that many dictatorial rulers still try to sneak a polytheistic ethic into a monotheistic moral universe. This polytheistic ethic is found in the doctrine of strict obedience to the ruler. If you wish to see a perfect example of this, listen to the modern-day theologians of Madkhali and Jami Islam who, while they do not say the ruler is Divine, tell you the ruler is *Divinely chosen*. It is the same dynamic save for the conclusion. It is a polytheistic mythological process that appeals to elements that cannot be accounted for through human reason or action. That God chose the ruler is an appeal to a mythology that is ultimately unprovable. You cannot contest it. You cannot rationally challenge it.

Every prophet coupled the message of monotheism with the struggle against injustice. This is core to the message of every single prophet. No prophet came to say, "I teach monotheism, but I also teach you to submit to injustice." Yet something remarkable distinguishes the career of the Prophet Muhammad. At this stage, humanity had matured to a certain level. It had passed through the Greek, Roman, and Egyptian experiences. It had passed through Hindu and Buddhist mythologies. With a living, preserved text—the text of the Qur'an—humanity had now reached a level of literacy which, if compared to the time of Jesus or Moses, was previously non-existent. At the time of the Prophet Muhammad, humanity had developed its relationship to writing and language to the point that monotheism now had a fighting chance. Mythology could be defeated.

This speaks volumes to us throughout the Old Testament. Time and again, the prophets of the Old Testament say that there is only one God. I could cite one hundred passages or more to show how often this idea is emphasized in the Old Testament. There is no Trinity or duality. There is no mention of a son of God. Nevertheless, despite this, a pantheon of gods were worshipped throughout most of the history of ancient Israel. This is a historical fact.

The mythology of the three-headed godhead was well known in Hindu and Egyptian religion. It was anchored in Greek philosophy. Plato, for example, says that God consists of three. Christianity started with the message of *tawhid* and, for as long as Christianity was an Israelite religion, that narrative persisted. The polytheistic mythology of the three-headed god was adopted after Paul, the founder of so-called "Pauline Christianity," took the Christian message from the Israelites to non-Jewish populations. You can easily read this in modern scholarship. The Christian doctrine of the Trinity comprises three gods who are eternally and immutably equal. That is why it is a mystery. If there are three gods overlapping in powers and ability, how could they be one? For this reason, you can read as much as you want in Christian theology, but the ultimate conclusion is that the Trinity is a mystery. No one has been able to understand it, and no one will ever will, because it is a mystery that is fundamentally incoherent. The persistence of this polytheism reveals how even the modern mind is still attracted to some primitive mythologies. Even the modern mind wants to feel the warm comfort, undying love, and apparent sacrifice of a God who suffered and died for our sins. This is typical of ancient mythology. It is inconsistent with the idea of individual accountability, responsibility, and rationality.

Let me say what Muslims need to understand: Islam was a critical step forward in the history of humanity. Without Islam, Europe would have never experienced a Reformation or Enlightenment—not without Islam's deconstruction of mythology, reclamation of the rational God, and reclamation of the idea that when you submit to God, you submit to no one else. This is why it hurts so much to see modern Muslims make Islam stupid. Like the ancient world, I see them reducing Islam to a universal mythology. They make Islam irrational, fantastical, and irresponsible. They talk about how we must obey this and not disobey that because it is God's will. That is pre-Islamic mythology. It is what in Islam we call *jahiliyya* (a state of ignorance). It undermines the Islamic contribution to the progress of humanity. Humanity had to put Christian mythology aside to progress to rationalism. It would not have been possible otherwise.

Every week, there are developments that illustrate what Islamophobia is doing to us as Muslims: concentration camps for millions in China; the increasingly horrible oppression of Muslims in Kashmir; India passing a law that allows political asylum and eventual citizenship for every religion except Islam; the continuing atrocities against the Rohingyas. Added to this is something more local and personal to us: Trump signing an executive order in which the American government intervenes in an area that no government has a right to intervene in. This requires understanding Title VI, a statute that prohibits educational institutions from discriminating on the basis of race, ethnicity, and national origin. But Title VI does not say anything about religion. So, Title VI allows universities to discriminate on the basis of religion. For a long time, whenever universities sought to invest money in studying the Israeli occupation and subjugation of the Palestinian people, Islamophobic and Zionist organizations would complain of anti-Semitism and work to ensure that that university lost federal funding. They did this if the university focused on the Palestinian plight or supported the Boycott, Divestment, and Sanctions (BDS) movement.

In other words, the same Zionist and Islamophobic organizations that claim that Muslims do not understand the value of freedom of speech themselves censor speech by qualified academics when they research Palestinian refugee camps, the number of Palestinians in Israeli prisons, or the number of Palestinians murdered by the Israeli army every week. They say it is anti-Semitic.

Trump signed an executive order that says that, for the purpose of Title VI, Jews are a nationality, not a religion. It blows your mind. How is it constitutional for the federal government to intervene to define a nationality and a religion? Trump did this, however, because Islamophobes lobbied him to pass the executive order so that any university that does not study Islam in the "correct" way—meaning in the Islamophobic way—or that criticizes Israel for its abysmal human rights record and its colonization of Palestinian land can lose Title VI money. Here, Islamophobes have no problem with censorship.

One would think that this would ignite a fire in Muslims' hearts to start putting their money where their mouth is to fight such an incredible threat to our academic freedom, the future of Islam, and the future of our children at American universities. But what hurts even more is this: where are those people from Zaytuna College who defended Trump? Where is the professor from Zaytuna who defended the Muslim ban?[55] Where is Hamza Yusuf and his serving on the U.S. government-affiliated Human Rights Commission?[56] Where are their voices and why are they so spineless? Why do they bring Islam back to the mythology of the deity-king? Why do they bring Islam back to *shirk?* The gift of Islam was the liberation from mythology, irrationality, and subjugation. That is what lit the fire under Islamic civilization. Why are modern Muslims killing our religion and bringing it back to the stupid mythology of the ancients who did not believe in personal responsibility and accountability?

I close with this. Someone recently wrote to me and asked, "What do you think is the single most important factor for the spread of Christianity, after colonialism?" In other words, exclude the power dynamics, and consider what is the biggest factor that made Christianity spread in various parts of the world, especially in Japan, Korea, the Philippines, and Africa. I thought about it long and hard. My answer? The image of a White Jesus. Jesus is represented in every image since Paul as a cute, good looking White man. Images of Jesus in churches look nothing like his description in the Bible. What if Jesus was depicted as the Palestinian from Galilee that he actually was? The hearts of many women and men melt over Jesus—the White Jesus. The image of the White Jesus conquered the world because racism conquered the world. Until you learn to be proud of your race, you cannot begin to understand why Jesus is never represented in the way that he is described in the Bible. In

---

55 On 6 June 2019, 'Abdullah bin Hamid Ali, a senior faculty member at Zaytuna College, rationalized the ban in a post on his Facebook account, claiming, "to be fair, a real Muslim ban would mean that no Muslim from any country should be allowed in the U.S. There are about 50 Muslim majority countries. Trump singled out only 7 of them, most of which are war-torn . . . So, it is unfair to claim that he was only motivated by a hatred for Islam and Muslims."

56 See The Usuli Institute, *Khaled Abou El Fadl on the U.S. Commission on Human Rights* (Excerpt, 12 July 2019).

a future *khutbah*, I will talk about Jesus and his appearance in the Bible.[57] I will compare it with all known images of Jesus, except for in the Ethiopian Church. Even in the Coptic church in Egypt he looks like an attractive, young, European male. That surprised the person who asked me. But think about it.

13 December 2019

---

57 See Chapter 14: *The Symbolic Caliphate and Returning the Gaze* in this volume.

14

The Symbolic Caliphate and Returning the Gaze

$\mathcal{E}$very period of Islamic history has its challenges. We start by underscoring the basic and unwavering truth that our entire existence has an Owner and a Maker, our Lord, and that we are but guests in this world. We possess the power to honor ourselves or to demean and debase ourselves. We are responsible for our actions and intentions. Accountability is the first principle of justice, and our God is a just God who holds each individual accountable for what they have committed, intended, and achieved in their lifetime.

Recently, there was an Islamic conference in Malaysia, with Turkey, Iran, and several other Muslim countries in attendance.[58] Saudi Arabia and the UAE vigorously protested the conference. Saudi Arabia also pressured Pakistan to abstain. I spent some time listening to the conference proceedings. I was struck by how painful it was

---

58 A reference to the so-called "Kuala Lumpur Summit" that took place in Kuala Lumpur, Malaysia, between 18–21 December 2019.

THE PROPHET'S PULPIT

to listen to. This is not because there was something wrong or even condemnable in what was said. The conference was painful because it reminded Muslims of the facts of life. As you would expect, the conference talked about the atrocities that continue to be committed against Rohingya Muslims by Buddhists in Myanmar, and the extent to which the world is complicit and disinterested. There is also the plight of Uyghur Muslims by atheist persecutors in China, which is beyond comprehension. It is quickly approaching the scale of the Holocaust. The evidence is undeniable. The number of Muslim lives and even organs that are being exploited is overwhelming. Chinese authorities actually harvest the organs of the Muslims they execute.[59] In a world that claims to be civilized and to have finally seen the light on universal human rights standards, it is overwhelming. But it does not stop there. Consider the desperate plight of Muslims by Hindu persecutors in India. Amid ongoing protests in India, many Muslims have been arrested and tortured in prisons. Consider, too, the persecution of Muslims by other secularized and westernized Muslims. Those in the Emirati, Egyptian, or Syrian governments are Muslim in only the most superficial sense. They may claim a Muslim identity, but they target and persecute any manifestation of Islamicity that they find objectionable, often under the banner of fighting "terrorism."

We also have the persecution of Palestinians in Israel. Not a day passes but Palestinians are arrested or killed, their homes are destroyed, and their lands are confiscated. The plight of Palestinians continues unabated and even deteriorates as we have a U.S. administration that simply does not believe in Palestinian rights and has adopted a thoroughly racial perspective, relegating Palestinians to a

59 See footnote 30.

130

subhuman category. It is as if they do not count. It is as if millions of Palestinian refugees around the world simply do not matter.

We cannot say the picture is complete without mentioning the reality of systemic religious bigotry in the allegedly enlightened, sometimes-Christian West. I refer to the reality of Islamophobia. The number and rise in hate crimes against Muslims in the West is consistently under-reported. Work with law enforcement and you quickly realize that this form of bigotry is endemic. Any identifiable Muslim who is stopped by a police officer in the U.S. should feel at risk of being the victim of a horrible act.

There were many presentations in the conference on the need for economic development and for Muslims to unite to develop an effective response to the genocides in China and Myanmar, to what is becoming a genocide in India, and to the rise of Islamophobia around the world. Muslims have become the most targeted religious group in the world. The only reason this does not strike us is because Muslims neither control nor are well-represented in human rights discourses. If we were, it would be public knowledge that no group today is as vilified and targeted as Muslims. Instead, we have a global propaganda machine that, for the most part, ignores the persecution of Muslims. Human rights organizations that do bring attention to the persecution of Muslims are not insiders to the Muslim voice. These organizations, even when supporting Muslims, are often detached and lack a sense of passion and real cause on behalf of Muslims.

There are two things to highlight from the conference. The first is a sad but undeniable reality that we as Muslims must confront. Notice that Saudi Arabia did not attend the conference. I suspect we all know why. It is because Saudi Arabia's policies, like that of the UAE, have become thoroughly subservient to the strategic goals of the U.S. and Israel. We must confront the reality that Saudi Arabia has abandoned even its symbolic leadership of the Muslim world. Saudi policies have become clear: it is only interested in a Muslim world that is thoroughly subservient and dependent upon whatever represents the strategic interests of the West. There is no desire at any level to assert autonomy or self-determination. The conference in Malaysia clearly reflects this new historical reality. The Muslim world today is without even a symbolic leader. Egypt, which at one time played an important symbolic role in leading the Muslim world, is no more. The UAE is more Christian than Christians, more Jewish than Jews, more Buddhist than Buddhists, more Hindu than Hindus, more Zionist than Zionists, and more Western than the West. Saudi Arabia, other than fighting Shi'a Muslims and stymieing Iranian influence, has become an absent player.

The second point is that it is time that we Muslims learn from the historical realities of the world we live in. I must admit that I have become increasingly convinced that we need to advocate, strategize, and think about the prospect of the rebirth of the Caliphate. Not an ISIS or Boko Haram-style Caliphate. Rather, a symbolic Caliphate that has a U.N. status as a demilitarized political organ with land, space, and a symbolic religious role, and that is considered a sanctified place. Imagine something close to the legal status of the Roman Papacy in international law. I realize that I am opening myself to floods of attacks and criticism, but it is due time that we Muslims wake up and face the reality. Without even a symbolic advocate on our behalf, an advocate that speaks in terms of a Muslim polity in the U.N. and elsewhere, that is not interested in buying Western weapons or in expanding territory or wealth, we will remain lost in modernity. It is due time that our intellectuals stop dancing around the issue and call a spade a spade. For that is the reality in which we live.

I recently watched an interesting movie, *Bombshell*, about sexual harassment at Fox News. One statement in the movie gave me great pause. It was when a Fox news anchor says, "Jesus is White and Santa Claus is White." This, of course, reminded me of how I closed my *khutbah* last week.[60] As expected, there were many responses. People were intrigued, offended, and scandalized. Yet it seems there is a great deal of interest in these issues in the Bible. Why is Jesus depicted as White? We know historically that Jesus was a Palestinian Jew from Galilee. There is nothing remotely White about him. He would have looked like a modern-day Palestinian or a Sephardic Jew. Yet the image of Jesus as a White person is among our earliest images of him. This is because of a simple but uncomfortable truth: for as long as it was a Jewish movement, Christianity did not spread. It is, in fact, problematic from a historical point of view to claim that Jesus intended to give birth to something called Christianity. From a historical point of view, the likelihood is that Jesus was a Jewish reformer. He was an Israelite preaching to Israelites. From the Muslim perspective, Jesus was a prophet of God who advocated a message first to the Israelites, then to the entire world.

Christianity spread to a limited extent in Persia, Arabia, and India. For a variety of reasons, however, this is not what made Christianity the religion that it is today. Christianity truly spread only after it was Romanized. What made Christianity the religion it is today is that it spread in what was the then-Roman Empire. The Roman Empire ultimately adopted Christianity as its official religion and coerced pagans to convert. That is why I chuckle when Christians claim that Islam was spread by the sword. For Christianity did not spread and would have never been established without the massacres of pagans,

---

60 See Chapter 13: *Liberation from Mythology and the Power of a White Jesus* in this volume.

from Egypt to Germany. The Christian slaughter of pagans in Egypt is a story in itself. It is interesting that Christianity did not come to a place like Egypt from Palestine. Rather, it came to Egypt from Rome. In other words, it is accurate, in my view, to say that Christianity did not "Christianize" Rome. Rather, Rome "Romanized" Christianity. This is why the earliest extant manuscripts of the Bible are in Greek and then Latin. Not enough Aramaic copies survived.

From a historical perspective, the Roman state adopted Christianity as a religion because it had a powerful message that served those in power, namely, it preached obedience. "Because Jesus died for your sins, your perspective or attitude to those in power is that they are God's will."[61] Remember that Rome at the time was confronting huge pagan rebellions. Rome realized what many leaders in authoritarian states realize: if you control the religion, you control the people. A religion that tells you the ruler is God's will, like the Wahhabis of today, is a very convenient religion.

This is the story of Christianity and the birth of the Church. While Rome embraced Christianity as the religion of the empire, at the same time Rome could not conceive of a God that looked anything like the people it had subjugated and dominated, i.e., a Jewish Jesus. From this emerged the erroneous image of a White Jesus, which was then transplanted elsewhere. I have visited more churches than you can imagine all over the world. The only exceptions I have found are in Africa where Jesus is African. In the same way that many do not understand the difference between imperial Islam

---

61 The point here is that the Christian belief that Jesus died for our sins emphasizes the sinful nature of humanity, as seen in the doctrine of original sin. The state therefore encourages the believer, because of their sinful nature, to focus on eternal salvation in Jesus, rather than on political matters or injustices. Consider the great wealth, power, and influence of the Catholic Church throughout history, which would not have been possible but for a close relationship with, even tolerance and assistance by, the state.

and the Islamic faith, many do not understand that Christianity, including Catholic, Protestant, and evangelical Christianity, has been interconnected with issues of race and ethnicity since its inception. Like all defeated cultures, many in the colonized world think the way to solve an inferiority complex is to imitate those who are recognized, consciously or subconsciously, as superior. That is why the English or French languages are symbols of prestige and spoken all over the world. Think about how small France or England is on a map. It is not because French is an inherently superior language to Swahili. It is because France, as a colonial state, was the dominant and superior culture to be imitated. Those who insist that Jesus is White should study history. So many people who embrace Jesus embrace him as an image of the superior colonial culture. I invite my Christian friends to adopt a critical attitude toward the racialization of images in their theology. Insist, as a Christian, that Jesus was Middle Eastern, Palestinian, a Jew, and try to understand the discourses of Jesus from that perspective rather than from the perspective of a White man.

An interesting book, *The Bible and Colonialism,*[62] explores in a very learned way the role of the Bible in anchoring the colonial reality of our modern world. Colonialism cherry-picked the Bible to perpetuate the White Jesus and the colonial project. This is similar to how most Christians today never read the Bible from cover to cover or memorize it. They read selections from the Bible. Attend a church service today and you are handed selected excerpts. The excerpts in the U.S. are different to those in Egypt, Uganda, or wherever. In the U.S., the excerpts make you feel sweet and nice. They talk of love and make you feel fuzzy. The excerpts in Egypt are different

---

62 Michael Prior, *The Bible and Colonialism: A Moral Critique* (Sheffield, England: Sheffield Academic Press, 1997).

and often include verses in which Jesus warns against falling prey to pagan influences, by which Egyptian Christians mean Muslims.

It seems you gain a new audience when you talk about the Bible. Someone wrote to me saying that the various languages of the Bible do not alter its message. Allow me to respond. First, an enormous number of Biblical manuscripts have been found to date, and no two manuscripts are identical. Second, if you do not think that translating from Hebrew to Greek, Greek to Latin, and Latin to English changes the message, then you do not know any of these languages. Indeed, you simply do not know languages.

Take something as simple as the fact that nowhere in the Bible does Jesus say, "I am God." Any semi-educated Christian will concede this. This doctrine was eventually deducted by the Church, but it is not found in the Bible itself. The typical response in Christian commentaries is to say, "Jesus did not want to say, 'I am God,' because he was afraid that the Israelites would kill him." But this raises the issue that, according to Christians, Jesus wanted to be crucified to die for our sins. Why, then, would he be afraid when he in fact wanted to be crucified?

Let us put that aside and consider the expression "Son of God." In Aramaic, one says *bar elaha*. What does this mean? Think of the Arabic term *birr al-ilah,* meaning a servant of God or someone in consistent service to God. Various tribes in the Old Testament are called the "sons of God" (Hosea 1:10; Jeremiah 31:9; Genesis 6:2; Deuteronomy 14:1; Exodus 4:22-23). In Hebrew and Aramaic, the expression "son of God" is akin to the Arabic phrase, "You are my son" (*anta ibni*). It does not mean that you are actually my son. Rather, it is an idiomatic way of saying, "I care a great deal about you."

In Greek, this was translated as *paies theo*, which can mean either servant or son. When the Greek was translated into Latin, a choice had to be made. The Greek description of the Prophet David as *paies theo* was translated into Latin as "servant of God," not son (2 Samuel 7:5). Indeed, even on Jesus, we see in Matthew 12:18 another example where the same word, *paies theo*, has been translated as "servant": "Behold my servant with whom I am pleased, my beloved one in whom my soul rejoices, and I will put my spirit upon him, and he will preach justice to the people." Return to the Greek manuscripts: *paies* was translated as "servant," not son. A choice was made in Latin that "servant" is a more fitting translation. We do not know what the text said in Aramaic because the Aramaic manuscripts are not extant.

Consider another example. Acts 3:13: "The God of Abraham and of Isaac and of Jacob, the God of our fathers has glorified His son, Jesus, whom you delivered upon and denied in the presence of Pilate when he was determined to let him go." Notice that in this verse the word *paies* has been translated as "son," not servant. Or take Acts 4:27: "For truly, they assembled in this very city, together with both Herod and Pilate and with the gentiles and with the people of Israel, against your holy son Jesus." We see the same thing. But notice, too, the language of "holy son"—the word "holy" here first appears in Biblical manuscripts in the fifteenth century.

One final example. The doctrine of the Trinity itself does not appear in any of the early manuscripts of the Bible. There are some examples of something that comes close to what became the doctrine of the Trinity. Consider Timothy 3:16: "Truly great is this Divine mystery of righteousness. It is revealed in the flesh, justified in the spirit, and seen by angels preached to the gentiles, believed in the world and received up into glory." This passage seems to suggest that Jesus is Divine and it could be interpreted to support the doctrine of the Trinity. There is only one problem: Timothy 3:16 does not appear in any Biblical manuscript before the sixteenth century.

The Bible is a complex text. In many ways, it is a text for scholars. Unlike the Qur'an, which is memorized from the first to the last page, no one memorizes the Bible. Even if one sought to memorize the Bible, one would not know which version to memorize. It requires years of study to know the layers of discourse existing within the Bible. For precisely this reason, there are Christians who believe in the Trinity and there are others who believe in duality: God and God's son. This, of course, has its own problems. There are Christians who believe Jesus was simply a prophet. They remain Christians because they do not believe in any religion after Christianity. This is to say nothing of the hundreds of sects and theological debates that have arisen throughout Christian history because of the complexity of the Biblical text itself.

20 December 2019

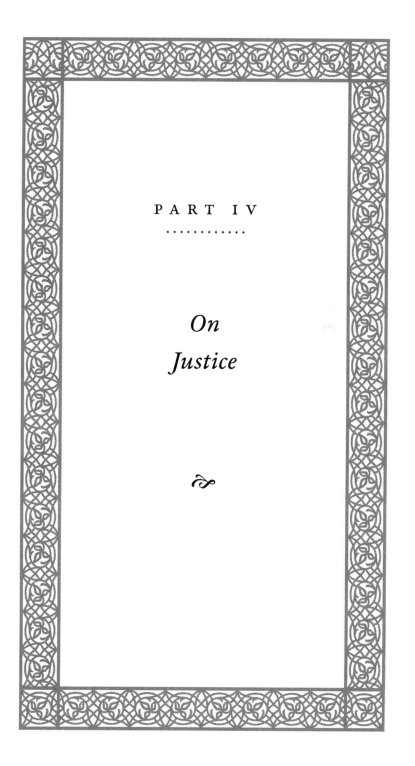

PART IV
· · · · · · · · · · ·

On
Justice

15

On the Definition of a Scholar

God reminds us in the Qur'an that God has given us a *Shari'a*, meaning a path or a way. God instructs us to follow this path, to pursue it, and to not deviate from it (Q 45:18); in effect, to not follow other leads or digressions that take us away from the path. This begs the question: what type of path is befitting the Lord and Maker of the heavens and the earth? What type of path is so worthy and important that we are eventually held to answer for it, and our very salvation or damnation depends upon the way that we handle our journey through it? Many think this path is something as simple as a set of positive laws. This is because they either have weak souls, weak spirits, or lazy intellects. It is elementary in the study of *Shari'a* that positive laws are only half the process. Any practice decreed by law must have a purpose. If the positive practice of the law does not lead to the purpose, there is a breakdown in the relationship between the lawgiver, the law, and the receiver of the law. Put differently, regardless of the positive legal commands that we follow—the specific *harams* or *halals*—if we do not understand *why* we follow the command, or *how* it fits within the *Shari'a* or the path of God, there is a fundamental breakdown.

Let me expand upon this. I submit to you that the earliest Muslims understood that, at a most basic level, the message of God is a message of liberation and moral and ethical progress. This is a common theme to all the prophets. It cannot be that God simply decrees a bunch of positive commands—"do not drink alcohol," "do prayers," and "fast Ramadan"—without these serving a larger purpose. Islam would have failed a long time ago had the early Muslims believed that God simply decrees positive laws that command us to pray, fast, or refrain from certain things, with nothing else to offer humanity. When you study the *Sira* (biography of the Prophet), you find the disciples of the Prophet were animated, energized, and excited about a moral vision, not simply a system of practice. We hear of Companions going to Africa and Asia and spreading the message of Islam wherever they went. If it was purely about rituals, no one would have been excited about the Islamic message. The Islamic message would have been no different than the countless other ritualistic creeds that came and were practiced in human society, before eventually disappearing. The moral vision that animated the Companions and Muslims throughout history was a moral vision of human dignity and liberation. It is summed up in that simple phrase: there is no god but God (*la ilaha illa Allah*).

In the pre-modern world, there were corrupt social structures in which an elite controlled resources and a clerical class served the idols that people worshipped. This clerical class extracted sacrifices from the poorest elements of society in order to appease the idols and enrich the aristocracy. The entire social system was thoroughly abusive. Into this came the Islamic liberation. The liberating message of Islam declared to both rich and poor, Black and White, free and slave: "Your dignity stems from your Maker. Worship your Maker alone. In the eyes of God, money does not belong to whoever controls it. Rather, it belongs to God, and you are simply deputies in charge of wealth on God's behalf." It was a revolutionary and liberating message. The earliest Muslims believed that the *Shari'a* of God broke the yoke of submission, empowering people to assert their humanity and to stand tall in dignity against those who controlled, dominated, and abused human beings. This explains the excitement of the Companions.

Look at the remarkable language in the Qur'an that teaches us about our moral trajectory on earth. God tells us:

> *So be steadfast, as thou hast been commanded—and*
> *those who turn in repentance along with you—and be*
> *not rebellious. Truly He sees whatsoever you do. And*
> *incline not towards the wrongdoers, lest the Fire should*
> *touch you—and you will have no protector apart from*
> *God. Thereafter you will not be helped. And perform the*
> *prayer at the two ends of the day and in the early hours*
> *of the night. Truly good deeds remove those that are evil.*
> *This is a reminder for those who remember. And be thou*
> *patient. Truly God neglects not the reward of the virtuous.*
> *So why were there not among generations before you those*
> *possessing merit, who would forbid corruption upon the*
> *earth, other than a few of those whom We saved among*
> *them? Those who did wrong pursued the luxuries they*
> *had been given, and they were guilty. (SQ 11:112-116)*

It is as if God is sketching an entire philosophy for us. It is as if God is saying, "Do not surrender. Do not allow yourself to be subjugated and dominated by the unjust." To not surrender to the unjust is a revolutionary message. And God knows that resisting submission and degradation is a difficult task. It requires moral courage to live a life in which you say, "I cannot coexist with injustice. I will not allow myself to be the servant of the unjust in society." The moral strength to do that requires daily and nightly prayers. That is why God then tells us, "And perform the prayer at the two ends of the day and in the early hours of the night" (SQ 11:114). For to reach the point in which you only fear God requires a praying soul. It requires a soul with an intimate relationship with God. It requires a praying soul to internalize the revolutionary idea that you should fear only God, not other human beings. Following this, God reminds us of the importance of patience: "And be thou patient" (SQ 11:115). The *Shari'a* is a difficult path. But it is not difficult because you are required to perform ritualistic acts. It is difficult because if you refuse to submit to the unjust, you will lose many of the privileges of this world, if not worse. So have God inspire your strength and patience. If it were an easy task, you would not need patience.

We then receive a remarkable reminder that God tells us is a cosmic law:

And thy Lord would never destroy the towns unjustly,
while their people were reforming. (SQ 11:117)

Which societies succeed and which societies fail? God tells us clearly that societies in which a critical mass of people aspire to establish justice succeed. If that mass does not exist, societies are destroyed. They are destroyed on account of their injustice. To put it bluntly: unjust societies are doomed, while just societies will thrive.

It is a beautiful, systematic, and earth-shattering discourse from our Lord and Maker. It teaches us what the path of the *Shari'a* is.

This is exactly why Islam was revolutionary and why every prophet came with a revolutionary message. From Noah to Abraham to Moses to Jesus, every prophet said, "Fear God and do not fear anyone but God. You are responsible for justice in society." If a critical mass of people works against corruption and oppression, God will help, and these societies will thrive. In the absence of this critical mass, societies are doomed. They are doomed by their own injustice and oppression. The Prophet tells us in a *hadith* that there are seven categories of people whom God protects in the Hereafter by casting a Divine shade upon them, which is a metaphor to mean that one is in the special care of God. The first of the seven is a just ruler.[63] The Prophet also tells us that the greatest *jihad* is to say a word of truth before an unjust ruler.[64]

Reflect upon this. In earlier times, it meant that you would travel, receive an audience, stand before the ruler, and speak a word of truth against the oppressive ruler who would then likely imprison or kill you. That was deemed the greatest *jihad*. That was a special category of people whom God cares for in the Hereafter. It is pedantic to think that applying this *hadith* in our age means taking a plane, driving a car, and somehow gaining access to an unjust ruler to speak to their face. In our day and age, we perform the greatest *jihad* through modern means of speaking to unjust rulers, which includes social media and print publications. It is through all the modern mechanisms that human beings, with God's aid, have created for discourse. But why does this matter so much? It matters

---

63 Bukhari (660) and Muslim (1031).

64 A widely reported *hadith* found in al-Tirmidhi (2174), Abu Dawud (4344), al-Nisa'i (4209), and Ibn Majah (4011-12).

lest Muslims slump back into a state of moral and ethical lethargy. If no one is willing to speak for truth and pay the price for truth, then you do not have narratives of bravery and struggle. If you do not have narratives of bravery and struggle, then people eventually lose sight of the importance of high principles. If people lose sight of the importance of high principles, then they eventually forget what the *Shari'a* is all about. They eventually think that the message God sent to Noah, Abraham, Moses, Jesus, and Muhammad is about ritualistic practice. They forget that if this were the case, Islam would have never had the influence that it had upon the world.

Here in the United States, you find so many sons and daughters of Jewish families whose pride and joy is to travel to Israel. Some of them have served in the Israeli army. Some have helped Israeli settlers steal Palestinian lands. This is a moral mission for them. Unfortunately, it is an oppressive moral mission for they are destroying an indigenous people, but it is a moral mission, nevertheless. So many children of Mormons will travel to Brazil or Venezuela to work for and spread the Mormon religion. Every other church has an evangelical program in which the youth proudly travel to Africa, China, or Haiti to do missionary work. Where are Muslims in all of this? Our organizations are ashamed to engage in, or to admit engaging in, anything close to missionary work. All we as Muslims want is to be accepted. "Please, please, just accept us as fellow human beings." In other words, we are weak. It is as if we have concluded, "All we want is that you allow us to do our prayers and fast in Ramadan." What is the result? I recently read a study that said that by the third generation, whether among immigrant or African American Muslims, in most cases, a sense of Islamic identity in the U.S. has been lost. If I am a Muslim, for example, perhaps I can raise my child to be Muslim. But my grandchild, the child of my child, will not be Muslim. Why? Because we do not understand what our *Shariʿa* is about, so we do not give our children anything to get excited about.

For several centuries, since the colonial period, there has been a consistent attempt to define the appropriate space for Islam. Muslims have in response developed certain themes: themes about *hijab*, themes about prayer, and themes about not envying others. Muslims have been repeating these themes ad nauseam for several hundred years. It has been a disaster. Attend any Islamic center, conference, or *khutbah* and, if you have been Muslim long enough, you can predict what will be said. Yet we cannot talk about the same things, in the same order, with the same logic, and in the same language for several hundred years, and not lose people. It is contrary to human nature. God created human beings with an innate sense of what is just and unjust, an innate sense of human dignity and relevance, and an innate sense for creative and imaginative energy. If every Islamic discourse fails to engage our creative energy or our sense of justice and dignity, what happens? If every Islamic discourse engages only the same themes in the same language, people will eventually say, "Islam has nothing to offer." Then, especially for Muslims in the West, by the time we reach the third generation, they are no longer Muslim. I cannot blame them. They seek a life that is nuanced and complex and they find Islamic discourses static and frozen. This is a very serious issue.

Who, then, has the primary responsibility to think and talk about the *Shariʿa* in a way that presents moral leadership to Muslims and humanity? It is, obviously, those who study the *Shariʿa*, the scholars. But what happens when our scholars lack moral vision? What happens when our scholars are behind the times because they read books written in the medieval age and have little knowledge of the modern world? What happens when our scholars say nothing new because they only imitate? What happens when our scholars are moral cowards and do not practice the greatest *jihad*? They do not stand before an unjust ruler and say, "You are unjust," just to make a point and be an example unto others. What happens is that the entire *Ummah* becomes exactly like them. If your scholars are cowards, you will be cowards, and you will inevitably lose your children because cowards do not lead the world. People who lack imagination, creativity, and daring do not lead the world. They are subjugated by the world.

The Orientalist dogma about "political Islam" is among the greatest disasters inflicted upon modern Islam. It was invented by an Orientalist French scholar, Olivier Roy, and Muslims then embraced it—because Muslims imitate whatever is given to them. If what is intended by the term is the idea that scholars should never rule in God's name, then I agree. This is valid and important. Scholars should not rule in God's name, for many reasons. However, if what is meant by "political Islam"—and, sadly, this seems to be the case—is the idea that scholars should not speak out against injustice, then scholars have lost the very reason for their being. If you cannot offer moral leadership, moral vision, and moral progress, you should stay quiet and stay at home. You have no role. If you claim to be a scholar in *Shari'a* but your position is one of silence before injustice, then it is as if you have said, "Yes, I am a scholar, but I am too much of a coward to perform the greatest *jihad*." Know that it is your right as a layperson to see those who position themselves as scholars aspire to perform the greatest *jihad* and to not be among those who surrender to the unjust. If they do not practice what the Prophet lauded as the greatest *jihad*, then they do not deserve your respect or reverence. God may tell someone who is a layperson,

"You are excused. You were busy raising your children," but they, as scholars, have no excuse.

During the time of the Prophet, there were those who went out with the Prophet to confront the enemy. There were others who stayed behind (Q 4:95). There were yet others who said that they were too busy with their businesses or families to join the Prophet (Q 48:11). There were all types of excuses. See what the Qur'an says about those who failed in their obligation toward the Prophet (Q 48:12-13). If scholars become among those who stay behind and prefer earthly achievements and pleasures, fearing the unjust instead of fearing God, and failing to set a moral example in the greatest *jihad* by speaking the truth, then you should not believe them when they say they are scholars. Put them aside for they do not provide moral leadership or a moral example. Say, "You are a coward, and a coward cannot lead an *Ummah*." Again, in our day and age, what is demanded of scholars is that they use modern means for speaking the truth. Do not let anyone tell you that to care about justice is "political Islam." The main function of someone who claims to be an expert in the *Shari'a* is to be a moral example and vision unto others, to represent moral progress. If instead they are cowards and their conduct exhibits all the symptoms of fearing human beings over God, then immediately know that they are a bad example. They are among those who have surrendered to injustice. They have become part of the formula that will lead to the destruction of the nation by its own injustice.

This is a critical *khutbah*. The primary role of a scholar is not to teach you how to pray or the rules of fasting. In our age, we can find most of this on the internet. The main role of a scholar is to be a leader, an example of how to fear God and no one else and how to establish justice through fearing God and no one else. In other words, the role of scholars is to testify. Testify against the oppressor in favor of the oppressed. Testify against injustice in favor of justice. Testify through performing the greatest *jihad*: speaking the word of truth. If they are too cowardly for this, then they should stay at home, and no one should listen to them. This is our *Shari'a*. This is our path. This was the path that was decreed to Noah, Abraham, Jesus, and Muhammad.

We talked a while ago about the video in which Hamza Yusuf mocks the Syrian revolution.[65] He cites the weak *hadith* that says, "Whoever insults a ruler, God insults them." It is a weak *hadith* that also reveals a remarkable lack of knowledge of the *Shari'a*. For the *hadith* is talking about a *just* ruler, not simply any ruler. The same applies to *hadith*s that describe the Sultan as "God's shadow." I raise this again because of an alarming phenomenon. As you well know, this video emerged before it was quickly taken down. Every time someone put it up, it was taken down. I have friends who tell me that the orders for taking it down came from Hamza Yusuf's students. Others say the UAE played a role in taking the video down.

What most concerns me is not even what was said, but the moral cowardice in taking the video down after it was posted. It tells you that Hamza Yusuf did not change his ideas. He still teaches the same material to his students—but behind closed doors. This is exactly the pedagogy and methodology of the UAE, which funds both Hamza Yusuf and many Muslim institutions in America. It is to teach quietism, political cowardliness, and a lack of moral vision—but behind closed doors. It is to influence the minds of the young without having to answer for the corruption of the doctrines that are being taught. What is my point? There are clear indications

---

65 See TRT World, *Hamza Yusuf under fire for comments about the Syrian revolution* (YouTube, 11 September 2019).

that, due to funding by the UAE and Saudi Arabia, our children are being taught behind closed doors to not care about justice. They are taught that we should simply obey a ruler, even if the ruler is unjust, and that we should not be politically active, even against something like the Muslim ban.[66] People send me emails, telling me, "We learned in our Islamic institute the *hadith* that says we must obey the ruler, whoever he or she is." I receive emails from students telling me that they are taught in Islamic institutions in the U.S. that it is *haram* to protest Trump's Muslim ban; they are taught that the ban was really about immigration, not Islam, even though the Supreme Court readily admits it is a deeply Islamophobic act because of everything the Trump administration said during the ban.[67] As a result, Syrian refugees come to this country, and who takes care of them? Christian families and churches. Muslims are not at all involved in caring for refugees. I find out that behind closed doors Muslims are taught that they deserve to suffer because they rebelled against their ruler.

A scholar must be brave. If a scholar says something, they must know what they are saying and be prepared to defend it. To say something and have it taken down while continuing to teach it in private is moral cowardice. It is a clear example of precisely what is wrong with our institutions. Let me be blunt: any scholar who accepts Emirati, Saudi, Egyptian, or even U.S. government money is not worthy of the name. Any scholar who tells you, "I teach something, but I do so in secret so no one can challenge me," is not a scholar. I

---

66 See footnote 53.

67 On 26 June 2018, the U.S. Supreme Court upheld the validity of the Muslim ban in a 5-4 vote split along ideological lines, claiming that the ban fell within Presidential powers and that this was not undermined by Trump's history of making inflammatory statements about the alleged threat posed by Muslims to the United States.

heard Hamza Yusuf's "apology." It is not an apology at all. I know he still teaches the same nonsense.

The fate of our Islam depends on every one of us. If you want to teach that Islam is simply about saving yourself from Hellfire by fasting and prayer, go for it. But let me tell you: your children or the children of your children will not be Muslim because you have nothing to offer them. If you still want to consider moral cowards as your scholars and examples in life, go for it. I have done everything I can. But understand the state of Muslims around the world. Christianity is spreading in Asia and Africa. Even the Mormon religion has spread in South America, Africa, and Asia. Look at how Jewish communities are raised with a cause and a purpose, even if it means stealing the lands of an indigenous and oppressed people. Meanwhile, our children are not raised with any moral vision or purpose, and you will not get your children excited about a faith that is simply about fasting and prayer, because you are not even telling them *why*. How does it make any difference in the universe?

Our children intuitively know who is a coward, and who is not. You cannot lie to them. No matter how many times you tell them to respect a coward, they will not. Even if they smile and say, "Yes, Mama. Yes, Baba," they will not respect a coward. And the price for that is Islam itself. You will have to answer for that before God on the Final Day.

4 October 2019

16

The Higher Aspirations of Justice

*... who shun grave sins and indecencies and who when
they are angry, they forgive, who respond to their Lord
and perform the prayer, their affair being counsel among
them, who spend from that which We have provided
them, and who, when tyranny befalls them, they defend
themselves. The recompense of an evil is an evil like unto
it. Yet whosoever pardons and sets matters aright, his
reward is with God. Truly He loves not the wrongdoers.
And whosoever defends himself after having been wronged,
for such there is no way against them. There is only a way
against those who wrong people and behave tyrannically
upon the earth without right. For them, there shall be a
painful punishment. And whosoever is patient and forgives,
that is indeed a course worthy of resolve. (SQ 42:37-43)*

These verses from Surah al-Shura lay out nothing less than a social, moral, and ethical constitution. The Qur'an manifests the power of words. Words make a great difference because of the way that God created existence. God created human beings as intelligent animals capable of reason and reasoning, and intelligent and rational animals respond to words. If you reflect upon the Qur'an, you find it consistently calls us to reason (Q 4:82; 12:105; 13:3; 45:13; 47:24). The earmark of the human species is that we are capable of reason, and the way to reach reason is through the power of words. The more that human beings stop responding to words, the more that words lose their place and role in our life, the more dehumanized we become. God created the universe and affects creation through the power of words. For something to come into being, God says, "Be" (Q 2:117; 3:47; 3:59; 6:73; 16:40; 19:35; 36:82; 40:68). The most miraculous thing about human beings is our ability to decide upon our path after having comprehended the power of words. What makes us accountable before God is either our willingness to respond to words, or our refusal and obstinace before words.

Reflect upon the rather obvious point that without words, there is no accountability. In law, you cannot hold someone to account without notice. Uttering the words that constitute the law creates responsibility and accountability. God reaches us and creates the entire mechanism of responsibility and accountability through the medium of words. Words are revelation. If God puts us on notice through the power of words but we no longer respond to words—meaning words no longer have any impact—then the entire mechanism for discharging our covenant before God falls apart. Indeed, the very logic and reason behind the process of creation, responsibility, and accountability falls apart.

In Surah al-Shura, God puts us on notice. God describes a people who are fully aware of their covenantal relationship with God and who successfully discharge this covenantal relationship. God tells us these are people "who respond to their Lord and perform the prayer" (SQ 42:38), meaning they are fully aware of their responsibilities before the Most High. They know prayer is a mechanism to acknowledge the ethical issue of gratitude to God. Following this, in the same verse, God addresses the social ethics of those who are rational and in a state of grace with their Lord: ". . . their affair being counsel among them, who spend from that which We have provided them" (SQ 42:38). This means they conduct their affairs through a system of *shura*, and that money is not hoarded and coveted but in fact circulates among them.

What is *shura*? "Consultation" does not even come close to the idea. A better word is "deliberation." *Shura* means that affairs are deliberative. So, *shura* is the power of words. It means "they share words with each other." Now, if a group "shares words" but then ignores each other, this is not *shura*. If the deliberative process is purely formalistic, this is not discharging the obligation of *shura*. There are debates in Islamic law as to whether the effects of *shura* are binding or not. But this is a legalistic and technical topic. I focus here on the social ethics of rational Muslim human beings. God reminds us that those in a state of grace with God conduct their affairs deliberatively, and that this deliberative process leads to the circulation of wealth. Money is not coveted or hoarded. There is no sharp inequity between rich and poor.

God quickly reminds us in the very next verse: ". . . and who, when tyranny befalls them, they defend themselves" (SQ 42:39). Take these words seriously. Can we say that a society is in a state of grace with the Lord if injustice occurs and there is no way to defend oneself? No. A society in which rights, boundaries, and territory can be violated without means of redress is not a blessed society. The problem is that we do not take the words of the Qur'an seriously as rational animals. A society in which there is an elite that rules like Pharaoh, with no deliberative processes, unjust wealth distribution, and no means to address or defend oneself against injustices, cannot, by definition, be an Islamic society.

Surah al-Shura goes to greater philosophical depths. It tells us that, as a principle of justice, wrong must be addressed proportionally and measuredly: "The recompense of an evil is an evil like unto it" (SQ 42:40). In other words, there must be a mechanism to address wrongs in a proportional fashion. If one person commits infraction X and is punished with ten years, for example, and then a second person commits the same infraction but serves one year, and a third person commits the same but receives twenty years, this is not proportional justice. This is not recompensing an evil with "an evil like unto it." So, the mechanism of justice in a moral and ethical order is not simply deliberative or distributive. The ability to address injustice must include the logic of proportionality, balance, and consistency.

Beyond the formal process of justice, moreover, the Qur'an addresses the idea of forgiveness. Here it speaks to individuals: "Yet whosoever pardons and sets matters aright, his reward is with God. Truly He loves not the wrongdoers" (SQ 42:40). After creating the formal means to address injustice, if one chooses to forgive, then it is between them and God. As if to make the point abundantly clear, however, God then says: "And whosoever defends himself after having been wronged, for such there is no way against them" (SQ 42:41), meaning that we are not to be blamed if our response to injustice is to do whatever is necessary to end the injustice. "There is only a way against those who wrong people and behave tyrannically upon the earth without right" (SQ 42:42). God is orienting our attention again. It is as if God is telling us—again, through the power of words—that if we want to be in a state of grace and meet our moral obligations before God, there must be mechanisms to address the unjust and those who transgress the rights of others.

With words like these, how is it that injustice, political cowardliness, despotism, nepotism, and all types of evil "isms" are so prevalent in Muslim lands? God makes it clear that we only attain a state of grace with God if our affairs are deliberative, if there is distributive economic justice, and if there are mechanisms to address injustice, compel the powerful, and empower the powerless. God clearly tells us that these are the rules of the game. How, then, can it be that in Muslim lands there are those who say, "Obey the ruler even if he flogs your back and steals your money," and who philosophize injustice, oppression, and despotism? How can it be that the mechanisms and institutions of justice in Muslim lands are so backward, reactionary, and undeveloped? How can it be that in Muslim lands the fields of engineering or medicine are perhaps developed, but discourses on justice and the institutions of justice are so undeveloped? To this day, I find it shocking when I hear Muslims say, "We need economic development." "We need engineers." "We need computer scientists." "We need doctors." Yet they are ignorant of advances in the field of justice. It does not even occur to them that the greatest challenge facing any society is to build institutions of law that create systems of equal accountability for the weak and the powerful. Whether in the West or the Muslim world, our thinking on such matters as distributive justice or the mechanisms and institutions of law is so backward. It is fair to say that we have attained zero development.

The *Sunna* of the Prophet was to give *khutbah*s that related to the living affairs of his community. Those who give *khutbah*s today on topics that have nothing to do with the living challenges of the *Ummah*, such as how to prepare for Ramadan or how to perform ablutions, do not follow the Prophetic *Sunna*. They follow the *Sunna* of despotism.

It is tragic that we live in an age in which Muslims ignore the magical power of the words of the Qur'an. Muslims have set aside the discourses on deliberative, distributive, and procedural justice, claiming instead that whoever holds power has the right of obedience. Many Muslims have read the Qur'an and Surah al-Shura time and again. When the institutions of deliberative, distributive, procedural, and substantive justice are undeveloped in Muslim societies, however, it means there is a cognitive problem between the reader and the text. In other words, God is speaking but no one is listening. If no one is listening, the result is precisely the mess that we see in our modern age.

In the Arab world, the ruler of the UAE, Muhammad Bin Zayed, is a devil. He is involved in everything harmful to Muslims. Muhammad Bin Salman and 'Abdul Fattah al-Sisi are also devils. It is fair to conclude, then, that an Islam that legitimates and justifies the ugliness, cruelty, barbarism, autocracy, and despotism of these rulers has killed the Qur'an. Regardless of whatever *hadith*s they claim to rely on, they have murdered the Qur'an. You can either read the *hadith*s, *Sunna*, and *Sira* in light of the moral guidance of the Qur'an, meaning that you interrogate that tradition in light of the ethical universe of the Qur'an, or you end up with a paradox that cannot be reconciled. For there are narratives of despotism in the tradition that create reactionary and backward mentalities that cannot possibly aspire to the type of moral universe the Qur'an challenges us to create. This is the moral universe of deliberative justice, distributive justice, procedural justice, and substantive justice.

There are many reasons, among them colonialism, why countries like Saudi Arabia, the UAE, Egypt, and Libya are the way they are. There are, sadly, many powerful people who want Israel to be the only democracy in the Middle East. They do not want a democratic Arab world. They see democracy or any form of justice in the Arab and Muslim world as a threat to Israel. Unfortunately, these wealthy and powerful people are thoroughly convinced that to give Israel the moral high ground, Israel must always be able to say to the West, "Look, we are the only good guys in this part of the world." Were another country to build a democracy and deny Israel that claim, it would somehow endanger Israel. Many powerful people think this way, meaning there are many reasons why the Muslim world is the way it is.

But what I cannot understand is when Muslims in the West ignore the moral universe of the Qur'an, producing an Islam that is about nothing more than meaningless rituals that do not lead to the liberation of human beings, the aspirations of justice, or to a higher ethical existence. Instead, this Islam teaches that your attitude toward this world must be one of bitter perseverance and patience, as this world is an evil place that must be endured before reaching the Hereafter, where the fun begins. Those who teach this kind of Islam not only create abnormal psychologies. They create sad, despairing, and bitter human beings who have big chips on their shoulders. They not only create the "opium of the people." They make Islam truly a system of darkness, backwardness, and reactionism. When religion becomes a vehicle for taking human beings to the depths of darkness instead of elevating them to a higher ethical plane, it becomes evil and harmful. If we are God-fearing Muslims, that is something we cannot accept about our faith.

I recently received a message from a friend who works in the field of human rights. He sought my help. One month ago, an Egyptian man named Ahmed Sabiʿ was arrested and disappeared. I had never heard of Ahmed Sabiʿ, but I spent several hours researching who this man was. I discovered that Ahmed Sabiʿ is a scholar of comparative religions. He is a brilliant young man who has perfected Hebrew and Aramaic. He uploads YouTube videos about ancient manuscripts and forgeries in the manuscript traditions of the Old and New Testaments. He posted a set of videos in which he teaches Hebrew to Arabs. He has studied the Talmudic tradition. He engages in discussions about the history of the Church and studies the Qurʾan and the Bible comparatively. In a set of videos, Sabiʿ responds to attacks on the Qurʾan by evangelists and Islamophobes.

I went through the videos and I could not figure out why the Egyptian government would arrest him. He does not talk about politics. He does not talk about Sisi. He does not talk about the Egyptian revolution, Saudi Arabia, or the UAE. All he talks about is the Qurʾan, the Old and New Testaments, and the history of comparative religions. Then, finally, I found a video where he referred to a recent video in which a woman grabbed the Pope's hand and pulled him toward her. In response, the Pope slapped the woman's hand until she let go. The Pope later apologized. Ahmed Sabiʿ showed the clip and, making a rather obvious point, said, "Compare this to what happened with the Prophet." When a woman grabbed the Pope's hand, he slapped her hand away. Meanwhile, in a *hadith* report, we read that the Prophet was walking in a market when a man grabbed him by his collar and yanked him so hard that it left a mark on his neck. The man yelled at the Prophet, "Give me some money." The Prophet turned around and smiled.[68] Ahmed Sabiʿ said the Pope reacted inappropriately, comparing it to the Prophet's response. He then said, "It is unfair that Islamophobes immediately celebrated the Pope's apology while relying on, focusing on, and criticizing anything negative in Islamic history." I discovered upon further research that some Christians in Egypt complained that Sabiʿ criticized the Pope for slapping the woman's hand. For that reason, he was arrested.

I have never met Ahmed Sabiʿ. I had not even heard of him. But this is what compels me to talk about justice. It is when a young man of that level and intellect, who has mastered Aramaic and Hebrew, is arrested for doing what all of us, without a second thought, can easily do, which is to criticize the reaction of the Pope. God knows what has happened to him. Look up Ahmed Sabiʿ and see his picture. Imagine what could be happening to this man. He looks like a decent, kind, and quiet human being. In all his videos, he never raises his voice. I then think to myself that there are still many Muslims who think we should not talk about injustice or despotism. What are they going to tell God? The arrest of someone like Ahmed Sabiʿ is the arrest of every intellect in the Muslim world. In the same way that God tells us that to kill one human being is to kill all mankind (Q 5:32), to arrest a single intellect is to arrest the scholarship of an entire *Ummah*. For it is to arrest the principle of the word and to pre-empt and abort the possibilities of justice.

I do not see Islam when I see that the reaction of Muslims in the face of injustice is to say, "That is just the way things are." That is not Islam. As far as I am concerned, the prayers and fasting of those

---

68 Bukhari (3149) and Muslim (1057).

who hear about the arrest of someone like Ahmed Sabiʿ and who continue with their lives as if nothing has happened are worthless. At a minimum, if we cannot do anything, let our hearts condemn it. For if even our hearts do not condemn it, there is no faith. At a minimum, if you find someone speaking out, do not discourage or silence them.

God challenges us to establish justice and to overcome injustice and aggression. God challenges us to institute justice through its various branches: deliberative, distributive, procedural, and substantive. God challenges us to do so as an extension of our covenantal relationship with God. For as long as we do not realize that Islam is, heart and soul, a rebellion against injustice, oppression, despotism, and suffering, then we have betrayed Islam itself.

7 February 2020

17

The Theology of Despotism and Reflecting on the Coronavirus

There is so much that takes place in the Muslim world every week. So much takes place in what is supposed to be a single *Ummah* bound by a common faith, a common cause, and a deep sense of compassion and empathy for one another. The Muslim *Ummah* embodies and represents Islam on earth. The very purpose, aspiration, and hope of this *Ummah* is to know God and to come to know one another through God. But knowing God is impossible without love and without loving God. Strict obedience, if unthinking and unfeeling, is a form of hypocrisy toward God. That obedience is a form of deception and lying; you are obeying because you are calculating the costs and benefits for entirely selfish, idiosyncratic, and narcissistic purposes. While that obedience is better than disobedience, it is not a lofty objective on the moral plane. If you do not learn to be truthful toward your Lord, you do not learn to be a truthful human being. A person who obeys solely out of fear is someone who lacks truthfulness and honesty, and who will not come to know the Lord.

To have a loving relationship with God, you must first commit yourself to an ethic of transparency and honesty about your relationship with God. You must commit yourself to something more than simple, blind, unthinking, unfeeling obedience. As an *Ummah*, that is supposed to be our aspiration. If we work toward that aspiration with sincerity, honesty, and truthfulness, seeking not just to obey but to please God, we learn to be truthful human beings and the bonds between the *Ummah* grow to become sincere and truthful bonds. The *Ummah* becomes accustomed to being truthful about itself and with itself.

So much happens every week that affects our *Ummah*. Yet, when you look at the discourses of this *Ummah*, meaning what it talks about, you do not get any sense of transparency and truthfulness. Indeed, it seems the *Ummah* is in a state of cognitive dissonance and collective denial. What the representatives of this *Ummah* talk about does not show any real engagement with either themselves, others, or, indeed, with God. How could it be that with all that confronts our Muslim *Ummah* in the modern age, you can go from one *jumu'a* to another and find that *khutbah*s speak of nothing that connects to the real world? Taking *jumu'a*s as a yardstick, it is no exaggeration to say that our *jumu'a*s exist in a state of complete artificiality; "artificial" in the sense that we talk about abstract ideas without attempting to relate these ideas to practical life. It is like trying to teach a child mathematics without any practical application; that child has never held little balls with which to count, so it remains an abstract intellectual exercise. Without being able to see the practical effects of mathematics, that child will never learn mathematics. The way our Muslim *Ummah* handles its discourses is very much like this. We talk of piety or justice, for example, but seldom attempt to demonstrate what the practical effects of piety and justice are, either in our relationship with God or in our practical lives. This state of artificiality has become a viral infection plaguing our *jumu'a*s and discourses. Ironically, it is the complete antithesis of the *Sunna* of the Prophet, which was a demonstrative example of how to practically apply the concepts of faith in our lives. Those who speak about the *hadith* and *Sunna* today often make no effort to follow the *Sunna* of the Prophet.

You cannot engage in self-determination without being honest with yourself, others, and God. Some of the most often-quoted and misrepresented Qur'anic verses that are used to teach Muslims the artificiality of religion, to disempower Muslims, and to rob them of their sense of self-determination, are found in Surah al-Nisa. These verses are wrongly used to teach Muslims that the way they practice their faith should be subservient to those in power; that those in power should decide all the material things affecting their life; that our job is simply to perform rituals without trying to turn these rituals into a means of empowerment; that self-determination and autonomy belong only to those in power.

> *God commands you to return trusts to their rightful owners*
> *and, if you judge between men, to do so with justice. Excellent*
> *indeed is the instruction God gives you. Truly God is Hearing,*
> *Seeing. O you who believe! Obey God and obey the Messenger*
> *and those in authority among you. . . (SQ 4:58-59)*

Hardly a week passes without hearing these verses—not the first part that speaks of ruling by justice, but the second part that speaks of obeying God, the Prophet, and those in authority. Time and again, whether we are dealing with Trump and his Muslim ban, Haftar in Libya, Sisi in Egypt, Muhammad Bin Zayed (MBZ) in the UAE, or Muhammad Bin Salman (MBS) in Saudi Arabia, in any context we can imagine, we hear our *imams* telling us, "Brothers and sisters, God told us to obey God, the Prophet, and the rulers." The implication is that obeying rulers is equal to obeying God and the Prophet.

If you ask, "But what is going on in the Holy Lands? How could it be that in the Hijaz, the land of the Prophet, there are now so-called "*halal* bars" where the likes of Mariah Carey, with her immodest, highly sexualized dancing, perform?[69] How could it be that UAE military officers torture, rape, and maim human beings in Yemen? How could it be that when the International Criminal Court demands that certain people be tried as war criminals, the rulers of the UAE simply refuse to discuss the issue?",[70] our *imams* respond, "Obey God, the Prophet, and the rulers. Do not ask questions. Do not talk about it in *khutbahs*. Do not raise any issues about what Saudi Arabia is doing in the Hijaz." The Egyptian government under Sisi has to date destroyed two thousand mosques and built five hundred churches. If you ask why, you receive the same response: "Brother, obey God, the Prophet, and the rulers."

This could be, theologically, one of the most important *khutbahs* that I give. For this interpretation of this Qur'anic passage is a total corruption of God's revelation. Every *imam* who cites this passage to justify injustice, suffering, inhumanity, narcissism, and the deconstruction of the Muslim *Ummah* is corrupting God's word. Let us consider the passage as a whole:

---

69 See footnote 37.
70 An allusion to the Libyan General Mahmud al-Werfalli. See Chapter 6: *Your Existence is No Coincidence* in this volume.

> *God commands you to return trusts to their rightful owners*
> *and, if you judge between men, to do so with justice.*
> *Excellent indeed is the instruction God gives you. Truly God*
> *is Hearing, Seeing. O you who believe! Obey God and obey*
> *the Messenger and those in authority among you. And if you*
> *differ among yourselves concerning any matter, refer it to*
> *God and the Messenger, if you believe in God and the Last*
> *Day. That is better, and fairer in outcome. (SQ 4:58-59)*

Consider the preceding statement: ". . . and, if you judge between men, to do so with justice" (SQ 4:58). If one rules or judges anything, it must be according to the principle of justice. That is the initial statement. Obeying God, the Prophet, and rulers comes second. The verse then refers to instances of disagreement. To whom does this refer? We would not, of course, disagree with God or the Prophet. If people disagree among themselves or with rulers, then, the constitutional reference is the principle of God and the Prophet. But we do not stop here. We do not selectively pick and choose from God's revelation. We continue with God's message. The very next verse tells us:

> *Hast thou not seen those who claim that they believe in*
> *that which was sent down unto thee and in that which was*
> *sent down before thee, desiring to seek judgment from false*
> *deities, although they were commanded not to believe in*
> *them? But Satan desires to lead them far astray. (SQ 4:60)*

Here the Qur'an talks about hypocrites. Why, and what is the cause and proof of their insincerity? It is because they seek the judgment of "false deities" (*taghut*). Their frame of reference is, ultimately, *taghut. Taghut* means despotism, injustice, oppression, deception, and lies. *Taghut* is every corruption.

God first tells us that our guide is justice; if we want to stay with God and the Prophet, our objective must be justice. We should in principle aspire to obey God, the Prophet, and those in authority. In cases of disagreement, however, there must be a method, procedure, institution, or instrumentality to resolve disputes so that *taghut* does not prevail. If *taghut* prevails in society, you are hypocrites.

There is another important point. God tells us to obey God, the Prophet, and "those in authority among you" (*uli l- 'amri minkum*). In the Arabic, *minkum* means "among you"—not "over you." In other words, there must be a process through which the ruler can legitimately claim to represent the will of the people. If the ruler does not represent the will of the people, they are not *uli l- 'amri minkum*. Rather, they are *uli l- 'amri 'alaykum*, meaning they rule "over you" (*'alaykum*) but do not represent you. God makes it clear in Surah al-Nisa, then, that those who rule over people must in fact represent them. Beyond that, God makes it clear that our compass in life must be justice. In cases of discord, *taghut* must not prevail.

I therefore say to all those pontificating and noisy *imam*s, from Libya to Egypt to Zaytuna College in the U.S., those who tell us to obey Trump because he is the ruler, "Sorry, but I do not obey despots. I do not obey tyrants. You do not understand God's book and God's command. God taught me that God and the Prophet are justice. Anything unjust cannot be from God and the Prophet. Anything that involves secret prisons, torture, sexual assaults, disappearances, and suffering cannot be part of God and the *Sunna* of the Prophet. Rather, it is from *taghut*, and *taghut* is from the devil. No to Trump, Sisi, Haftar, MBS, MBZ, and their despotism. They are all *taghut*. They are not *uli l- 'amri minkum*."

Understand this so that we stop corrupting our religion. Our religion never sanctioned despotism and tyranny. So-called *imams* who use God's book to undermine God's book should have no place among us. Make a difference by deciding which *imam* to follow and which *khutbah* to listen to. Choose which discourse to support. If you support *taghut*, the path of tyrants and oppressors, then you are among the *taghut*. You are part of the *taghut* problem, not part of the solution. So many issues confront our Muslim *Ummah*, and *taghut* is chief among them. It is the law of tyrants, despotism, suffering, oppression, and blind obedience. Know that the true path is one of thoughtful and loving obedience. "I will obey, but I must first understand. I will obey, but I must love. If you do not earn my respect, understanding, or love, I will not obey." That is how we resist *taghut*. That is how we raise our children to be proud Muslims.

So many issues confront our Muslim *Ummah*, but I would be remiss if I did not focus on an issue that has reached unbearable levels. Recently, there was a documentary on *Al-Jazeera* about the 1979 siege of Mecca in which Juhayman al-Otaybi led a group that believed in the *Mahdi* (the awaited Messiah), occupied Mecca, and took hostages. According to the Saudi government, after two weeks, Saudi forces eventually stormed the *Haram* and defeated the rebels. The documentary revealed that it was in fact French special forces, not the Saudi army, that broke the siege. For decades, there were rumors that the Saudis used French special forces, but no proof. *Al-Jazeera* produced the proof with the testimony of the very French soldiers who participated in breaking the siege. What most alarmed me and caused me to think of the nature of *taghut* was the Saudi claims at the time that three hundred people were killed. That number included the rebels who instituted the siege and the pilgrims who were taken hostage. We learn from the documentary, however, that no less than five thousand people were killed. I asked my Saudi friends, "Is it true that five thousand people were killed?" To my great chagrin and sadness, they told me they knew this long before *Al-Jazeera* broadcast the program. In fact, they knew that after French paratroopers broke the siege, Saudi forces could not discern rebels from pilgrims as people escaped the *Haram*. Saudi forces began shooting everyone to the extent that the French paratroopers begged them to stop the bloodshed. Saudi forces ultimately executed five thousand people inside the *Haram*.

This, in the sanctity of the Ka'ba. This is where the Prophet forbade even shedding the blood of an animal. I will not discuss whether the siege could have ended through other means. But I will address the fact that a government can kill five thousand people inside the *Haram* and there is no means to hold anyone to account or to even get to the truth. There is no means for investigation. There is a tyrannical government that does not allow an investigation. There is no way for the light to break the darkness. I ask you: is this not *taghut*? When there are lies and untruths, is it not *taghut*? When five thousand people can be killed and there is no way to know who did what, is it not *taghut*? Meanwhile, non-Muslims from France, who earned millions for their military operation, speak about how awful it was to see so many civilians executed.

Recently, a Saudi woman appeared in a YouTube video in which she tells us, "Listen, Muslims! Even if King Salman opens bars and nightclubs in Medina and Mecca, shut up and do not say a word. The only thing you are entitled to do is go to the Ka'ba, do your pilgrimage, and get out." In other words, it is none of your business for King Salman is the ruler and the ruler is owed obedience.

This is not our religion. It is not our religion when five thousand people are slaughtered and you are told, "It is none of your business, shut up." Or when people are tortured and raped in Yemen in secret prisons by Saudis and Emiratis, and you are told, "Shut up." Or when people are bombed in Libya and murdered in Syria, and you are told, "Shut up." Or when people are massacred in Rabaa in Egypt and you are told, "It is none of your business, shut up."[71] Nor is it our religion when the Muslim ban is expanded, and you are told, "Focus on your prayer. It is none of your business. Shut up." Is this not *taghut*? Does this not teach you to be a liar and a hypocrite?

Our Islam is about justice. Know that anyone who confronts injustice by talking about ablutions or supererogatory prayer is a hypocrite and part of *taghut*. They uphold *taghut* through their silence. To be silent before injustice is to be a "mute devil" (*shaytan akhras*).[72] Let me be very clear: I heard the late Jamal al-Khashoggi say in an interview that if we Muslims stop caring about what happens in Jerusalem, we will soon stop caring about what happens in Medina and Mecca; if we Muslims forsake Jerusalem, we will also forsake Medina and Mecca. He was talking about the principle of whether a human being cares about morality, ethics, and justice.

As I speak today, Saudi Arabia is arresting Palestinians. Why? Because these Palestinians have relatives in Gaza and these relatives

---

71 Egyptian security forces operating under the command of ʿAbdul Fattah al-Sisi killed over nine hundred protestors participating in a sit-in in Rabaa al-ʿAdawiya and al-Nahda squares, on 14 August 2013. *Human Rights Watch* has described the incident as a crime against humanity and as "one of the world's largest killings of demonstrators in a single day in recent history."

72 A reference to the famous statement, "The person who refrains from speaking the truth is a mute devil" (*al-sakit ʿan al-haqq shaytan akhras*). Both al-Qushayri (d. 465/1072-73) and al-Nawawi attribute this to the early scholar and Sufi Abu ʿAli al-Daqqaq (d. 405/1015). Islamic sources typically discuss this in relation to the Qurʾanic command to enjoin the good and forbid the bad (Q 3:104; 9:71) and the famous *hadith* of the Prophet: "Whosoever of you sees an evil, let him change it with his hand; and if he is not able to do so, then (let him change it) with his tongue; and if he is not able to do so, then with his heart," which is found in both Muslim (49) and al-Nawawi's collection of forty *hadith*s (34).

have other relatives that have been arrested by Israelis. The Palestinians in Saudi Arabia sent financial assistance to their families in Gaza. As a result, Saudi Arabia arrested them and charged them as terrorists. This happened this week. So, Jerusalem is gone, Palestinians are thrown into prison, and a brilliant young mind like Ahmed Sabiʿ remains in prison in Egypt for daring to criticize the Pope.[73] A Muslim in a Muslim country cannot carry out a comparative study of religions without being arrested. What is our collective reaction to all this in our *jumuʿas*? It is to talk about ablutions, piety, and fasting. That is *taghut*. It is the embodiment of *taghut*.

I want to quickly comment on the coronavirus pandemic that has hit the world. Look at the nature of our religion. Need I remind you that ours is the religion in which, one thousand four hundred years ago, the Prophet said, "If you are in a place that is afflicted by a plague, neither enter nor leave."[74] In other words: quarantine. Today, the idea of quarantine is unremarkable. But it is remarkable that the Prophet taught the procedure for quarantine all those years ago. When the Prophet was told, "But if we stay in that place, we may die." His response was, "Yes, you may die. But you are sacrificing yourself for the good of others and you die a martyr." Only a Muslim could be in a place in which a plague is spreading, and say, "I cannot hurt other human beings. I cannot put myself ahead of others and run away, sneak out, and spread the infection." Only a Muslim can say, "My religion commands me to think of the good of others, to love others, and to care about others. As a result, if I get sick and die, I die a martyr." Is this the religion of blind obedience? Is this the religion of idiocy, ignorance, and *taghut*? Islam taught

73 See Chapter 16: *The Higher Aspirations of Justice* in this volume.
74 Bukhari (5729).

the ethics of humanity long before philosophical ethics matured to what it claims to be today.

Many are asking if the coronavirus is a punishment from God. I do not know. But I *do* know that God tells us that hardship is an opportunity to reflect upon our faults and failures and work to improve ourselves (Q 2:155-157, 214; 6:42; 67:2). I therefore hope that the Chinese government and the rest of the world uses this opportunity to think carefully about the immorality of eating and mistreating animals. Chickens, pigs, and ducks suffer unbelievable cruelty in Chinese food markets. When an animal is terrified, it releases certain chemicals that poison the blood. As Muslims, God forbade us from eating terrified, mistreated, and tortured animals. God forbade us from eating fanged animals, like bats. I hope this is an opportunity for people to reflect upon the fact that they are not entitled to mistreat God's creatures under any excuse. Moreover, shortly before the pandemic, I was among those calling upon governments and companies to boycott China and Chinese products because of what the Chinese government is doing to Uyghur Muslims in East Turkestan.[75] The virus arrived and many of the companies that we called upon to institute a boycott terminated their trade with China. The financial losses upon China are far greater than anything that could have resulted from a boycott.

This virus is an opportunity to reflect and ponder. Whether it is a Divine punishment or not is not my business. But it *is* an opportunity to grow, improve, and to correct past sins and past mistakes. The same applies to all of us as human beings. When hardship and suffering afflict us, we can either crumble and go to the dark side, or

---

75 Also known as Xinjiang. Xinjiang is the official name of the region used by the Chinese government, its supporters, and most global media outlets. Many Uyghurs, however, refer to their homeland as East Turkestan.

we can use it as an opportunity to reflect, ponder, think about the path we have taken in life, and work to improve ourselves.

I dream of the day in which the way Muslims react to injustice, ugliness, oppression, and tyranny is that you could not attend a *jumu'a* anywhere in the Muslim world without hearing *imams* raising their voices, defending the oppressed, and speaking out against injustice. If that day comes, rest assured that God will be on our side. God will elevate us to the purified and loving state that God intended for us. Until we testify for God and justice, however, we will remain orphaned in the way that we are.

14 February 2020

PART V
. . . .

On Gratitude
and
Navigating
Hardship

18

When the World Goes Silent: Reflecting on Loss

L ast week, I was forced to cancel the *khutbah*. God bestowed
a gift that is both a challenge and a blessing. The gift is that
I lost my hearing. Whether it is reversible or not, we do not know.
In most cases, doctors do not know the reason for the sudden loss of
hearing. Nor do they have anything more advanced than cortisone
shots to attempt to bring life back into the fine mechanisms that
God has created to perceive and absorb sound. The ear is a truly
miraculous organ. The way in which very fine hairs move to interpret
waves to produce within the brain a comprehension of sound and
meaning is miraculous. It is so miraculous that God consistently
reminds us in the Qur'an that if we truly reflect upon ourselves,
we will see that everything we enjoy, even the most minor coordi-
nation, the simplest thought, the way we interpret every desire, is
clear proof of the Divine. The nature of human beings, however, is
to not reflect upon things until we lose them. It is to take blessings

for granted. Our very ability to express ourselves or to perceive the world around us is something that we do millions of times every single day, and yet we never pause to think of the sheer magnitude, majesty, beauty, and miraculous nature of the act. We can perceive, talk, hear, think, analyze, and taste every single moment of the day and yet still experience doubt about how much we owe God, if there is a God, and whether, in fact, this God cares or is involved. Even the way the simplest animal sees, hears, and tastes is a message to us of the miraculous, magnanimous, majestic, and subliminal.

It seems obscene to take God out of our lives, to enjoy or indulge every moment of every day, and continue with existence as if we owe nothing, as if there is no debt to pay, and as if we are not intimately an extension of the Divine. Hearing, seeing, thinking, and tasting are all Divine marvels. The question is: how do we navigate these marvels? Do we navigate them toward the fulfillment of the Divine or toward the fulfillment of the ungodly, demonic, and apathetic? Do we navigate them toward light or toward darkness? Things are not more complicated than this. We human beings are masters of distraction, diverting our attention from what really matters to avoid reflecting upon the constant marvels of Divinity with which we are intimately involved.

Your hearing stops, the world goes silent, and suddenly you start to notice what has been taken away. Whether God restores it is up to God. Results are always in God's hands. You do not hear a rooster at dawn. You do not hear the birds. In my case, all the concertos and sonatas that I dreamt of, thought of, and took for granted listening to time and again fall silent. It suddenly strikes me that I miss the sound of the *adhan* (call to prayer). I think of all the times the *adhan* would go off and, because I was busy working, I turned it off. What if for the rest of my life there is no more *adhan*? I think of how many times I had an opportunity to listen to my favorite Qur'an reciters. What if I spend the rest of my life and the only voice that I hear reciting the Qur'an is my own? I cannot resist the thought: what if my hearing returns? Will I be more attentive to the *adhan* and Qur'an? Will they be given priority, or will my old habits and weaknesses return? It suddenly strikes me that I cannot and will not hear my children say, "Baba." I suddenly miss that word so much. If God returns my hearing, will I be a more attentive father? Or when I would hear my wife calling my name and it irritated me because I was busy and wished to be left alone to finish whatever I was doing. Will I be a better husband if my hearing comes back?

Sit with God in a moment of truth and you realize that you are willing to promise God the world, if only God would return what has been taken. "I will be a better father, husband, and Muslim." But you know, deep down, that you are a liar and a hypocrite because you are weak. You know that you will not uphold your promises. You know that you will break whatever promises you made in your time of need. A wise person does not need to lose to wake up. A wise person does not need to experience loss to reflect upon their relationship with God. Most of us, however, including myself, are not wise. Most of us excel at diversion and distraction.

Every challenge is a blessing because every challenge is an opportunity to ponder, think, reflect, reform, change, and grow. Many people, when struck by a challenge, ask God, "Why?" It is a silly question. Instead, take the opportunity to reflect upon the ways that you may have failed yourself and consider the loss a moment to grow before your time runs out and you truly have no more opportunities to work with. Ask God to give you the strength of consistency to steer you away from the hypocrisy and hubris that gives you a false sense of immunity. Be grateful that God stands by you as you persevere through any challenge and loss. Make the sincere supplication, "God, help me grow from it. God, help me reach a higher state toward Your most sublime and most perfect Divinity. For there is no other guide and no other anchor in existence but You." We are in a constant state of grace and blessings. That we only become aware of these blessings after they are taken from us is somewhat vulgar and impolite. It is bad manners to the point that I feel embarrassed.

Last week, I was preparing to speak about something that, as Muslims, we cannot fail to speak about. I refer to the recent massacre that took place in Germany in which a man shot several people sitting in a hookah bar.[76] Before shooting Muslims, the man wrote a twenty-five-page manifesto. Of course, because Muslims remain compromised and powerless, I know they will not rush to read the manifesto to understand why such acts of violence take place and how they are connected to the world in which we live. The manifesto is deeply racist. It is a manifesto about the hierarchy of races that could have been written at the end of the nineteenth or early twentieth century. What is more dangerous is that this man reflects a growing phenomenon in the Western world. He represents the re-emergence of racist ideology that sees humanity as fundamentally unequal. According to him, certain races must be exterminated. Critically, this man talks about Islam as a race, not a religion. According to him, the world must rid itself of the "Islamic race," meaning Turks, Egyptians, Iraqis, Afghanis, and every other Muslim must be exterminated from the face of the earth. The man is also deeply anti-Semitic. He wants Jews exterminated. This is the nature of the game. Whether they realize it or not, pro-Israeli

---

76 A reference to the incident known as the "Hanau shooting," which took place on 19 February 2020 in the town of Hanu, near Frankfurt-am-Maim, after a gunman killed nine people at two hookah bars after expressing extreme right-wing views online.

Islamophobes who preach hate against Muslims are poking the same hornet's nest from which anti-Semitism and the Holocaust emerged. The same racist ideology that seeks to exterminate Muslims will not create exceptions for Hindus in India, Jews in Israel, or every other race that is considered "naturally inferior" to the White race. As is typical in these cases, the man decided to engage in this massacre as a symbolic act to awaken his fellow Whites to the necessity of "cleansing" violence so that Whites rid themselves of the "inferior races" among them. Also deeply troubling is that he even has a videotape, in English, which is a message to Americans. He is pro-Trump and urges Trump to lead the war to exterminate Muslims.

This occurred only one week ago, nine people were killed, and it is already old news. If the perpetrator of the attack was Muslim, there would be countless articles and books written about Islamic radicalism, Islamic violence, the Qur'an, and so on. Instead, it has been just one week, and it is already old news, labeled a common crime and the act of a deranged man. Trump did not even bother to condemn it. This is the same Trump whom Muslims at Zaytuna College support by working with his administration on a commission to re-examine human rights.[77] Racism is a monster. Racism is the deadliest disease in modern history. Racism is responsible for genocides, colonialism, and unfettered imperialism. Muslims should be at the forefront of the fight against racism, but they are not.

A clearly racist and Islamophobic terrorist attack occurs in Germany and no one talks about the Western philosophies responsible. No one subjects Daniel Pipes or Robert Spencer to scrutiny. Why? Because at this point, it is no longer just the evangelicals or Zionists who espouse Islamophobia. The most Islamophobic themes

---

77 See footnote 54.

are believed, repeated, and even acted upon by Muslims themselves. "Muslims only believe in violence and their entire theology and philosophy is about warfare." Who made this statement? The President of Egypt, 'Abdul Fattah al-Sisi, before the scholars of al-Azhar. It is repeated by the "educated" classes in Saudi Arabia, the UAE, Egypt, and all over the Muslim world. It has become an article of faith that Islam is defective and that we Muslims have something to be ashamed of.

Those of us who know better are in one of two situations. A scholar like Salman Alodah, who can respond to Islamophobic claims, is in prison. Yusuf al-Qaradawi, with whom I disagree on many things but who could respond to Islamophobic and racist prejudices, is isolated and muted. I recently saw a program on the Saudi *Al Arabiya* news channel that demonized and vilified a scholar like Tareq al-Suwaidan in Kuwait.[78] The program was thoroughly Islamophobic. It labeled him an Islamist who wants to institute the theocratic rule of the Caliphs, which is, again, a thoroughly Islamophobic trope. An impressive intellect like Ahmed Sabi', someone who learned Aramaic and Hebrew to engage in comparative religious discourse, is still in prison. I disagree with the Azhari *Shaykh* 'Abdullah Rushdy because he did not stand up to the military coup in Egypt that overthrew an elected government, which I think is sinful. Yet Rushdy is now banned from giving *khutbah*s, leading prayers, and faces criminal charges. What is his crime? It is that he said, "According to the Qur'an, you have to be Muslim to go to heaven." Whether you agree or disagree is not the point. The point is that he dared to express his opinion. For that, he faces criminal charges.

---

78 For more on Tareq al-Suwaidan, see The Usuli Institute, *Building Muslim Leaders with Dr. Tareq al-Suwaidan* (Conversation Series, 10 May 2021).

Think of the hypocrisy. Those who claimed that Muslims do not understand the principle of free speech when Nasr Abu Zayd was prosecuted or during the Satanic Verses affair are now completely silent.[79] 'Abdullah Rushdy is facing prosecution and they are silent. They may object to the imprisonment of Salman Alodah but they do not turn it into a matter of free speech. On Ahmed Sabi', there is absolutely nothing. When the persecuted are not even Islamists but simply those who defend an Islamic perspective, they are silent. At the same time, Trump can witness a racist attack and not even bother to condemn it. It is not even an issue in the presidential debates. Can you imagine if the victims were Jewish? Can you imagine if it was a Muslim who attacked a synagogue in Germany? Can you imagine how all the presidential candidates would be falling over each other to say, "We thoroughly condemn this"?

Brothers and sisters, life is in the hands of God. I feel that I am running out of time. I feel that my journey in this life has been one in which I have called, and called, and called, and those who responded to the call have been few. These are moral issues that will plague our children for generations to come. The Qur'an emphasizes belief, prayer, and the spending of wealth (Q 2:261; 2:274; 9:34; 49:15). Take away one of these three, and it does not work. Those with wealth should find, support, and fund the brightest intellects so that we can create a momentum against racism, Islamophobia, unjust imprisonment, torture, and the denial of due process. In other words, so that we can become a force against the abuse of power, injustice, and oppression. So long as Muslims sit on their couches, having only their rear ends grow and their weight increase, without

---

79 Many Western academics and journalists reported on the case of Egyptian scholar Nasr Abu Zayd who, in 1995, was declared an apostate in an Egyptian court for what was viewed as his liberal and critical approach to mainstream Muslim teachings.

taking responsibility for the world in which they live, then I am truly glad that I am deaf. For there is little in this world other than the Qur'an, the *adhan*, and classical music that I really want to hear.

28 February 2020

19

What Do You Hear When the World Goes Silent?

The Prophet Muhammad was a moral and ethical example unto humankind, like a beacon of light. Those who do not understand the moral guidance and example of the Prophet lose so much because they cannot truly be guided to the path of Islam. Glory be to God who gives and takes. Last week, I began the *khutbah* by sharing the news that I had effectively lost all my hearing.[80] I have now had several steroid shots in the ears and MRIs. I have met ear specialists and neurologists. I thank and praise God that I have not suffered a stroke and do not have a tumor. But sudden hearing loss is a reality. In my case, it seems it will be permanent hearing loss in which I suddenly enter a different category in life, from the hearing to the unhearing. It is the category of the functionally deaf. It is, of course, natural to reflect upon this loss. The nature of human beings

---

80 See Chapter 18: *When the World Goes Silent: Reflecting on Loss* in this volume.

is to not reflect upon something until we lose it. So many people do not reflect upon their families until they lose their families. So many do not reflect upon the blessing of a stable job until they lose their job and income. So many do not reflect upon the blessing that their children are safely asleep in the next bedroom and that they are not worried as to whether their children will be alive, abducted, or killed tomorrow. There are so many examples. We do not reflect upon something until we lose it.

Loss educates and humbles. There are those who lose something and become angry, asking questions that cannot and will never be answered: "Why me?" It is a selfish question. Why anyone else? The fact is that it *is* you and, since you have been chosen, what do you do with the loss? I am among those who never reflected upon the blessing of hearing. That is my fault. I often reflected upon the blessing of sight, taste, and even smell. But I always took the blessing of hearing for granted. This is until I was suddenly introduced to a bizarre new world, a world in which trees do not rustle and birds do not sing. People talk to you and you continue walking. You are not disturbed by the noise of music, radio, or television. The world is eerily silent. Something very interesting happens when the world becomes silent: you have to start listening. There is a voice within that you cannot shut off and that continues to speak in your head. It is the voice of the self. When the world becomes eerily silent, you confront the self. And when you confront the self, you start truly reflecting upon what you are made of. What does the self entertain and busy you with? You no longer listen to distractions. You no longer listen to stereos, radios, computers, YouTube, or nature. You listen only to the self. What does the self tell you?

This is the blessing of what God gives and takes. It is an amazing educational opportunity. It is an opportunity to listen to what will testify for or against you in the Hereafter. Every one of your senses will testify in the Hereafter (Q 36:65). Your eyes, ears, and hands will testify. Every part of your body will testify in truth and say, "This is what he or she did with us." This is an opportunity to hear that testimony before it is too late. When you listen to the self, it either exposes a petty, weak, anxious, greedy, short-sighted, and ignorant person, or it challenges you to rise beyond that and look into the self to find nothing but God, so that the voice that comes through the silence is nothing but the voice of God.

If the voice of God penetrates the silence, there is no moment of loneliness. There is not even a moment of loss. What loss could there be if silence only opens the door for the voice of God to come through more clearly, more purely, and more beautifully? There is no loss, only supernal beauty.

Reflect. Do not be like me. Do not wait until you lose to appreciate, reflect, and be grateful. Think of every sense that God has given you. Think of every moment you use that sense. How are you using your eyes, tongue, brain, hands, and feet? How are you using your stomach and ears? Are you using them in a way that will elevate or degrade you when they testify in the Hereafter? It is as simple as that. That is the power of religion. I have seen videos of those infected with the coronavirus who are so angry. They get on an elevator and lick the buttons, hoping to infect others. Or they spit on police officers or passers-by. Of course, if you think everything happens by chance, your response to an affliction will be, "Why me?" If there is no answer, you will say, "Why not share the misery?" Every person who has shot innocent people in public before killing themselves thinks that way. "I am miserable, let others suffer." "I am sick, why should I die alone? Let others die."

But what does religion do? Religion says that it is not all about you. Nor is it chance or happenstance. There is a God who sees you and holds you accountable all the time, everywhere. Religion says we cannot allow ourselves to fall to our basest level because we are elevated by the reality of the Divine. If religion does not do that, it is not religion. If it does not elevate us to beauty and make loss an opportunity for elevation, not degradation, it is not religion. This is the essence of everything. Thank God for what God has given and taken. Repeat *"Alhamdulillah"* for when you acknowledge your gratitude, you become aware of your faults and aspire to be better, and that is what God wants for us. That is why God told us that God does not accept *kufr* (Q 39:7), which means ingratitude. God does not want us to become ungrateful human beings because we then become ugly human beings. May God guard us against ugliness, especially ugliness in the name of faith.

It is critical that we remind ourselves that the essence of Islam is a message of mercy unto humankind (Q 21:107). This is particularly so in our day and age as we have become so confused about the message we carry to humanity. So many Muslims are unsure of what even something as simple as saying, "Muhammad is a moral example unto humanity," means. They say, "But I heard this in the *Sunna*; but I heard that. . ." Islam has been demonized around the world. It is as if the Bosnian genocide was not enough. Why did the Serbs slaughter and rape thousands of Muslims? It is because they claimed that Muslims are dangerous and that they need to protect Europe from the evils of Islam. At the time, some of us thought the Bosnian genocide was so horrific that nothing of the sort would happen again. Yet, we have seen the unbelievable genocide against the Rohingyas. The same ideological tropes used to slaughter Muslims in Bosnia have been used against the Rohingyas: "We are protecting ourselves against Islamic terrorism, violence, and jihadists." We witnessed another horrific genocide against Muslims in Chechnya to ostensibly "protect Europe from jihadists." We now witness the fate of the Uyghur Muslims in China. China's horrific concentration camps have been justified as a war against "terrorism" to protect China from jihadists. India's horrific war against Kashmiris is justified as a war against "terrorism" to protect India from jihadists. The fascist and nationalistic Hindu government in India has committed another massacre in Assam and is building concentration camps for Muslims, following China. All the material you read coming from the Indian government says, again, "This is necessary to protect ourselves from jihadists." But what hurts the most is when Saudi Arabia, Libya, and Egypt kill civilians left and right and say, "This is to protect ourselves against Islamic militancy and jihadists." It is against what they call "political Islam." The Saudi-UAE genocide in Yemen uses the same exact dogma that was used by the Serbs against Bosnians, the Indians against Kashmiris, the Chinese against Uyghurs, and the Russians against Chechens. I wish it was only the governments of Saudi Arabia, the UAE, and Egypt. But the problem is that these governments are served by an army of *imam*s that legitimate and justify their murderous and Islamophobic language.

The problem is that colonialism confronted an ideology of resistance within Islamic civilization, which was often called "*jihad.*" Colonialism did everything it could to demonize Muslim resistance and the language of *jihad.* The colonial propaganda machine came to say that resistance was wrong. As time moved on, rulers in Muslim countries realized that colonialism created two Islams: a quietist Islam that never resists, and a resistance Islam. The former is very useful for these rulers, while the latter is the one true challenge to their absolutism and despotism. Despotic rulers in Muslim countries are like Pharoah in the Qur'an, who tells his people they can only believe what he wants them to believe (Q 40:29). They prefer pacifist and quietist Islam. It is a blessing for them when a scholar is willing to be quietist and tell people, "Obey the ruler because obeying the ruler is equal to obeying God." If you are a scholar who talks about justice, fairness, equity, and social problems, however, you are part of the problem.

Reflect upon the fact that the elites in Muslim countries like the UAE, Saudi Arabia, and Egypt were not educated in Muslim institutions. Their political and social awareness was created by colonial institutions. They were educated by colonial powers. Whether in Russia, the U.S., or Britain, they went to elite schools where the professors were vetted through national security means. I know those who teach at naval, intelligence, and military institutions. Almost all these professors are thoroughly Islamophobic, and these professors have educated military officers in Libya, Egypt, the UAE, Saudi Arabia, Kuwait, and even Qatar. The way these leaders understand Islam, then, is through the eyes of the colonizer. They look at resistance as futile and stupid. They think only an idiot would resist.

That is why the fascist and nationalistic Hindu government in India does not bother Muhammad Bin Zayed (MBZ). That is why India can commit a genocide against Muslims and the UAE gives Narendra Modi an award.[81] It is because Hindu nationalism and political Hinduism do not bother MBZ like "political Islam." Sisi in Egypt is not bothered by political Judaism, militant Israeli groups, political Hinduism, or political atheism in China. He is not bothered that China massacres millions of Muslims. In fact, Sisi recently put

---

81 On 24 August 2019, the UAE awarded the Order of Zayed medal, its highest civilian honor, to Modi. The move came weeks after Modi's Indian government stripped Kashmir of its special autonomy, sent thousands of troops to the region, and imposed a strict military curfew.

Chinese flags all over Cairo and even projected Chinese flags onto mosques.[82] It does not bother him because Sisi's psychology is not the psychology of a Muslim. It has been ideologically and pedagogically constructed by the colonizer. That is why Muslims die in Yemen, Libya, and Palestine, and it does not bother these rulers. If White people die in Europe, however, they take note. This is our reality. This is why it hurts when I see people who should know better, who have some level of education, failing to understand the disaster of Muhammed Bin Salman in Saudi Arabia, MBZ in the UAE, or Sisi in Egypt. Think of the fact that I am banned from the Islamic Center in Southern California (ICSC) for speaking against Sisi.[83] The ICSC is supposed to be the cream of the crop. If so, then we are truly lost. What Sisi and his likes are doing to Islam and Muslims in the heartlands of Islam is causing damage that will last for centuries.

I want to share an interesting study that was released by the *Pew Research Center* on European attitudes toward religion.[84] Among other things, the study documents European attitudes toward Muslims. What I found most interesting was the following comparative question: would you accept a Jew as a member of your family as opposed to a Muslim? In the worst European country, the Czech Republic, only twelve percent said that they would accept a Muslim as a member of their family, as opposed to fifty-one percent who would accept a Jew. In the best European country, the Netherlands, eighty-eight percent said they would accept a Muslim as a member of the family, as opposed to ninety-six that would accept a Jew. In

---

82 In March 2020, the Egyptian government projected the Chinese flag onto multiple state and religious monuments as a proclaimed display of "solidarity" with China over the coronavirus pandemic.

83 See footnote 3.

84 Pew Research Center. *Eastern and Western Europeans Differ on Importance of Religion, Views of Minorities, and Key Social* Issues (29 October 2018).

most European countries, a majority of people said they would not accept a Muslim as a member of the family. Moreover, in every single European country, people were more likely to accept a Jew as a member of the family as opposed to a Muslim.

Yet, compare our discourses on anti-Semitism with those on Islamophobia. Compare the sensitivity of the Israeli government to any anti-Semitic act around the world with the "sensitivity" of the Muslim governments of Saudi Arabia, the UAE, Egypt, Kuwait, or Qatar to Islamophobic acts around the world. When anti-Semitism occurs, Jews are righteously and properly outraged. But Muslims? We say, "Well, maybe we deserve it. It is complicated. There are these bad Wahhabis and maybe they make people hate us." The study documents that anti-Semitism remains a problem in Europe. But the study clearly shows that Islamophobia is a far greater problem. Yet compare the number of studies and funding that an academic receives for working on anti-Semitism in Europe as opposed to those who write on Islamophobia. If I tell a publisher that I want to publish a book on Islamophobia, they will say, "Why? There are a lot of books out there. We do not need a new study." They would never say that about anti-Semitism. They would not dare.

The study asked whether religion is an important part of Europe's identity. Eighty-two percent in Armenia said it is important for Armenia to be Christian. In the most liberal country, Latvia, eleven percent said Christian identity was important. This is a study that included almost all European countries.[85] Between Armenia and Latvia, it is clear that a strong percentage in all of these countries,

---

85 The countries included were Armenia, Georgia, Serbia, Greece, Romania, Bulgaria, Poland, Moldova, Portugal, Croatia, Russia, Lithuania, Italy, Ukraine, Ireland, Belarus, Hungary, Switzerland, Austria, Spain, Slovakia, Germany, the United Kingdom, Finland, France, Netherlands, Czech, Norway, Belgium, Denmark, Estonia, Sweden, and Latvia.

in some cases a clear majority, consider religion core to European identity, that is, that Europe is Christian. Israel can be as Jewish as it wants. Even a sizable minority of forty percent in the Netherlands says the Netherlands should be Christian. The figures approach fifty percent in France and fifty-three percent in Italy. My point is that religion, even in the West, is a key component. It has not disappeared.

Now turn the gaze to the Muslim world. We apologize for our Muslim identity. We apologize for having a historical or an ethical identity that is anchored in the Qur'an and the Prophet. Our Muslim rulers think it is part of their liberal job to "renew" Islamic discourse and to say, "We are not really Islamic."

Let me close with this. Last week, the Muslim world lost an important man and scholar, Dr. Muhammad 'Imara. He was a very dear friend who was not only a great scholar, but also a great human being. He was on the Council of Scholars in Egypt but in all the years that I knew him, he never once made me feel inferior or as if he was speaking down to me. For many years, he would visit me and we would talk for hours. He published over one hundred books but lived with great humility. He never owned new furniture or even a car. I would beg to send a driver to pick him up because I did not want him to take public transportation. He was the epitome of a man who lived for the principle and idea of Islam. He had no material wealth but never took money from Saudi Arabia, the UAE, or the Egyptian government. As a result, he lived and died in poverty. When I lost my hearing, one of the first things I thought of was, "If I go to Egypt and cannot sit with Muhammad 'Imara to listen to him, it would kill me." Of course, I did not know that on that same day he was on his deathbed.

What most hurts is that Dr. Muhammad 'Imara was one of Islam's greatest intellectual gifts of the last century. He wrote extensively on

Islamic history. He edited and published the works of Muhammad 'Abduh (d. 1323/1905), Jamal al-Din al-Afghani (d. 1314/1897), and 'Abd al-Rahman al-Kawakibi (d. 1319-20/1902). Yet Muhammad 'Imara was banned in Egypt from publishing books, writing articles, appearing on television, and even posting videos on YouTube. After the military coup, he was thoroughly banned. Nawal El Saadawi, of course, could appear on Egyptian television and regularly curse the Prophet. But Muhammad 'Imara could not respond either in print or in the media. Yet there remain Egyptians who praise Sisi, and I am still banned from the ICSC because of my criticism of Sisi.

God has given you a brain. May God put you in the Hereafter with those whom you love. If you love the Prophet Muhammad, may you be with him. If you love Sisi, may you be with him. That is my *du'a'*.

6 March 2020

20

Trials of a Prophet Loved and the Mirror of the Coronavirus

God reminds us that if God allowed human beings to suffer the consequences of their actions, nothing would remain on the face of the earth (Q 35:45). Divine grace, blessings, mercy, and compassion intervene in our lives every minute of every day to save us from our follies and give every individual, even the most ungrateful, yet another opportunity to do good. God blessed humanity with a beautiful human being and a true moral example in the Prophet Muhammad. No Prophet has been as vilified throughout history as the Prophet Muhammad. Yet God reminds us of the basic truth that the Prophet was a man of great ethics (Q 68:4). It is because of his ethical character that he could bear the enormous burden of carrying the Qur'an. We also know in the famous *hadith* of 'Aisha that when asked about his moral character, her answer was simple:

his moral character was the Qur'an.[86] God reminds us that the Prophet was sent as a mercy unto humankind (Q 21:107). One of the things that God tells the Prophet has always melted me. To be honest, it often makes me jealous. God tells the Prophet, "You are in Our eyes" (Q 52:48). This is an Arabic expression to mean, "I love you to the point that it is as if you are in the core of my heart." One of my persistent supplications is:

> God, I know You said this to Your Prophet. You told Your Prophet that he is in Your eyes. That is how much You love and care for the Prophet. God, I know I am not worthy. I know I do not deserve it. But, God, please make me among those who are covered by that statement. I want to be in Your eyes, like the Prophet. I want to be that close to You. I want You to care about me to the point that I am in Your heart.

That same man, the Prophet, whom God addresses and tells him, "You are in Our eyes," was married to a lovely woman. Khadijah died and it broke his heart. He had a loving uncle, Abu Talib, and saw him pass away, after which he went through a truly difficult time. That same man, the Prophet, had to endure seeing two young sons, 'Abdullah and Ibrahim, die before his eyes. In other words, it is not an indication of God's love that God spoils you on earth. You can have horrible losses in life such as losing your children, wife, and parents, growing up an orphan, and losing your uncle, your protector and paternal figure. You can suffer all these calamities. What determines whether you are so close to God or removed from God is the way you handle these calamities.

---

86 Muslim (746).

I have been aching to talk about this as life runs by. One must think about what one wants to document and leave behind. What do you say so that it is at least out there? The key to loving the Prophet is to understand that this is a man who lost his mother and father as a child. His entire life was one loss after another. Throughout his entire life, however, there is not a hint of bitterness. There is not a hint of anger at the world. There is not a hint of anger at God. There is no hint of sociopathic behavior. There is no hint of a depressed, philosophically jaded attitude toward life. We know enough to know that it hurt him. The fact that he grew up an orphan hurt him. He missed his mother dearly. There was a maternal figure, a wet nurse named Halima, who took care of him when he was a baby. He cared about her and would even call her "mother." He continued to be remarkably compassionate and loving toward her. We know he cried dearly when Khadijah and his sons died. We know about his heartbreak. But it is what you do with calamity. It is how you react to hardship. It would have been easy for someone who loses his parents, wife, uncle, and children to say, "God does not love me. God does not care about me." But the reason the Prophet went through all of this is to teach us a lesson and to provide us with a moral education. We can go through a great deal of hardship, but we must keep our hearts pure. What keeps hearts truly pure is *dhikr*. "Are not hearts at peace in the remembrance of God?" (SQ 13:28) Remembrance of God brings comfort and tranquility to the heart. "And worship thy Lord, till certainty comes unto thee" (SQ 15:99). Continue doing *dhikr* until God sends you the strength to make you a solid human being who does not turn tragedy into an excuse for evil.

I say this especially to our youth and our ignorant Muslim masses. I receive so many emails from young Muslims, saying, "I heard this about the Prophet. How about this event? How about this incident? How about this? How about that?" Islam spread very quickly and, as a result, many people entered Islam who either did not understand Islam or who remained hostile to Islam and entered it for purely political and career reasons. Many *hadith* narrations were invented by those who pretended to be Muslim and who did not like the Prophet. Throughout the centuries, most of these reports went into quarantine. Scholars recognized these anti-Muhammad traditions that say horrible things about the Prophet and quarantined them. Both Islamophobia and Wahhabi-puritanical Islam have since returned to these *hadith*s and circulated them among Muslims once again. I can give you one example. There is a *hadith* report that claims the Prophet attempted suicide. Can you imagine? The tradition says the Prophet went to a mountain and was about to throw himself off it before the Angel Gabriel prevented him. For centuries, this tradition was quarantined. You could grow up, live, and die as a Muslim having never heard of this report. Today, however, this report has come out of cultural quarantine because Islamophobes and evangelists found it, said, "Wow. That makes Muhammad sound crazy," and publicized it.

But there is one big difference between the Muslim past and present. In the past, Muslim institutions were strong, while our Muslim institutions today are so weak. For that reason, we no longer control the discourse on Islam. We do not have the ability to quarantine things that should be quarantined. What we do have, however, is our mind and conscience. When we find God describing this man, the Prophet, as a man of great ethics (Q 68:4), as a mercy unto humankind (Q 21:107), and as so close to God as to be in God's heart (Q 52:48), that should be our yardstick as to what to believe about our Prophet.

Without the moral example of the Prophet, we Muslims have very little. My response to young Muslims who send me these messages is this: if you believe this, you should not be Muslim. If you really believe the Prophet did this, what kind of Prophet would he be? I do not need to enter a long scholarly discourse with you. This was a man more beautiful than Buddha, Jesus, and Moses. He was the most beautiful example unto humanity. Would you believe something ugly about him? If you do, then your Islam is flawed, and you need to reexamine your relationship with God. He was a mercy unto humankind. Mercy does not cause hardship. It does not cause pain. It does not commit ugliness. It does not do unethical things. For mercy to be comprehensible to human beings, it must invoke something intuitive and natural in us. So, when you see an *imam* acting in a way that strikes you as cruel, unethical, or ugly, and he tells you that it is the *Sunna* of the Prophet, you do not need to read Khaled Abou El Fadl to know this is wrong. You do not need to have read hundreds of books to be able to say, "No, I do not accept that. That is not the Prophet. I do not need books to tell me that you are not acting according to the *Sunna* of the Prophet."

We are all experiencing the coronavirus pandemic. Everyone is preoccupied. The story of the pandemic educates us. It teaches us a great deal about ourselves and the morality and immorality of our modern condition. It is a book of philosophical wisdom for those who wish to reflect. I want to highlight certain things. God tells us that it is God's *Sunna* to send or allow hardships to afflict a people so "that perhaps you may turn to God" (Q 6:42). We will not get into a philosophical discussion about causation, that is, whether this happens through direct intervention or the laws of nature that God allows to function. What matters is the response to hardship.

Turning to God means not just supplicating to God to remove the hardship. It carries the meaning of humble reflection. Let us humbly reflect upon what a not-particularly-lethal virus can do to humanity.

Reflect upon what we human beings can do to each other. We have perfected the evil of biological weapons. Our societies have allowed leaders to invest money not in health, education, feeding the poor, or helping the homeless, but in developing weapons that can wipe out humanity and that are far more lethal than the coronavirus. That immediately needs a pause. Yet God, through God's mercy, saves us from our follies (Q 35:45).

Second, God tells us that God made us nations and tribes so that we will come to know one another (Q 49:13). In other words, so that we will socially interact. We are so interconnected and interlinked today to the point that the eating habits of people in one culture thousands of miles away can affect all cultures around the world. Humanity today tortures and terrorizes animals before killing and consuming them. Terror and torture poison the blood of the animal. If these animals could speak, they would have much to complain about and a legitimate case against us for the suffering we inflict upon them before they die. They will do so in the Hereafter. God tells us to avoid consuming pork and animals with fangs and claws (Q 5:3). Shortly before the pandemic, I was working with a group to prevent some cultures from consuming dog meat. I still have the images of dog corpses hanging in markets imprinted in my mind. The way pork is treated before slaughter is inhumane and disgusting. We are so interlinked that the immorality of a particular market in Wuhan, China, can affect the rest of the world. We must exist in a world in which we can collectively prevent these immoral abuses. We are so interconnected that there is no such thing as, "That is their culture. It is their business." Each of us has a vested interest in everything, including our consumption habits.

Another lesson from the pandemic is the sinful way we treat the environment. We destroy the natural habitats of animals that live in forests. When these animals leave the forests that we destroy, they intermingle with human beings. When they intermingle with human beings, viruses such as the coronavirus come to be. God will hold us collectively responsible for what we do to the environment. This pandemic is a warning from God. A Muslim today cannot vote for someone without taking into consideration their stance on the environment. The environment is an Islamic moral and ethical issue. You do not have the liberty of not caring. It is an Islamic issue, and the pandemic is your warning.

Another lesson from the pandemic is that the global world order is deeply unfair. It allows permanent members of the U.N. Security Council to do whatever they please. Countries like China and Russia not only exercise the power of veto but can also ignore the procedures, treaties, and U.N. institutions that could have possibly prevented or responded to an outbreak like the coronavirus. The same applies to the U.S. The U.S. government can develop coronavirus tests and medicine but, as a world power and a permanent member of the U.N. Security Council, it is not obligated to share anything. The pandemic is a warning to humanity that this world order is unfair and immoral.

The lessons do not stop there. The pandemic reminds us that we live in a deeply racist and classist world. Look at how the coronavirus is so widespread among Syrian refugees, Palestinian refugees, in Sudan, and in Egypt. If those who get sick and die are in dark-skinned countries, however, no one cares. Their governments do not care, and we do not care. So, we do not count them. The World Health Organization has neither the jurisdiction nor the resources to go into these dark-skinned and underdeveloped areas to count the number of victims if their governments do not want it to count. Follow the daily counts. In White Europe, meaning France, Italy, Switzerland, and England, when someone dies, it matters. But in Africa? India? Thousands are dying and no one cares. No one counts. The pandemic is yet another reminder from God that we live in a deeply racist and a deeply immoral world system.

Another type of racism has emerged. There have been racist attacks directed at Asian people in England, the Netherlands, and even in Egypt. Let me be clear: you cannot be less Islamic. In Islam, even if you know your guest is infected, you cannot evict them. You cannot deny your neighbor help, even if you know they are infected. Your Islamic obligation is to put yourself at risk and let God take care of the rest. This is to say nothing of the stupidity and irrationality of targeting those who look Asian. Again, the pandemic is holding up a mirror, and saying, "Humanity, take a good look at yourself."

Lastly, the pandemic teaches us the evil of dictatorship and authoritarianism. No one knows how many have died or are infected in North Korea because North Korea is a dictatorship and it is the leader who decides. If the leader does not want anyone to be infected, he says, "No one is infected." It is the dictatorship in China that allowed the virus to spread out of control before the government finally relented and acknowledged the problem. That lack of transparency and accountability is the nature of dictatorship. Dictatorship makes us clueless about the true spread of the virus in Saudi Arabia. Not only do we not know, but we will never know. In Egypt, all the indicators are that Egypt has become a hot zone that exports the virus to the rest of the world. People returning to England from

Egypt have the virus. In the U.S. alone, we have people in New York, Texas, California, and Utah who were infected in Egypt. Twenty-two tourists from Houston returned from a Nile cruise in Egypt with the virus in what has been called the "Luxor Boat incident." Yet the government refuses to stop flights with China or Italy or close schools. It even arrests anyone who reports that their child caught the virus at school. There are reports that the government is burying those who die from the virus in villages in mass graves. The Egyptian government only acknowledges coronavirus cases in cases involving tourists or when the U.S. or British governments force it to do so. After the "Luxor Boat incident," the U.S. embassy forced the Egyptian government to conduct tests, even providing the tests, on all those on board the boat. It found that everyone on the boat, including the Egyptian crew, was infected. The Egyptian government, if left to its own devices, would never have done this. It does not care. Again, this is the nature of dictatorship. Egypt has become a hot zone, but dictatorship does not allow anyone to do anything about it.

Like all challenges, the coronavirus was not sent by God simply to wreak havoc. It contains lessons. Our job as Muslims is not just to follow our government's instructions and close our mosques and hide in our homes. It is to reflect upon what God is telling us. As a Muslim, you should protect yourself. But you must also take care of your neighbor. The idea that you have water and food but your neighbor does not is unacceptable. It is also your Islamic obligation to care for the sick. If you die, you die a martyr. But you cannot abandon the sick. If you really want to act in an Islamic fashion, buy masks, medical supplies, and tests, and distribute them in the poorest neighborhoods. The Islamic thing is not to just cancel *jumu'a*. It is to be God's *Khalifa* (deputy) on earth.

Wake up. Wake up before you find disaster and calamity and you have a great deal to answer for in the Hereafter when God asks you about these things. Did you condemn the dictator? Did you condemn the corruption? Did you condemn the lies? Did you recognize what is moral and immoral? If, by then, you have no answers, it will be too late.

13 March 2020

21

Perhaps You Will Turn to God: On the Coronavirus and God's Love

I am giving this *khutbah* in unusual circumstances. I want to start by explaining a few things that are important to understand. Scholars disagree on the number of people required for a *jumu'a* to be valid. Some scholars say you need at least seventy people. Others say one hundred and fifty. Others say twenty and yet others say a minimum of four people, other than the *imam*. Unless you reject that opinion, then, the number of people required for a valid *jumu'a* is four. For many reasons, I think this is the correct position for Muslims in the U.S. or in other countries where Muslims are a minority. Perhaps if we were in a Muslim country, I would not agree with that opinion. What this means is that you cannot have a virtual *khutbah* or virtual *jumu'a* unless it is based on an actual *jumu'a*, in which there are a minimum of four people, other than the *imam*, and the *khatib* follows the rules of an actual *jumu'a*. The rules for a proper *jumu'a* come directly from the Prophet. For a *jumu'a* to be valid, there must be a first *adhan* and a second *adhan*, a first *khutbah* and a second *khutbah*. Each *khutbah* must invoke praise and glorification upon God and the Prophet, as well as other rules. The reason I conduct a virtual *khutbah* is because it is based upon a valid physical *jumu'a*.

I mention this because I have noticed that some groups have decided to imitate me in holding virtual *jumu'a*s and virtual *khutbah*s, but these groups, sadly, know nothing about Islamic law and do not seem to realize that you cannot simply do things without understanding the *Sunna* of the Prophet and the jurisprudential evidence. I do not want people to rely upon invalid virtual *khutbah*s. If a man stands by himself somewhere and says, "I am doing a virtual *jumu'a*," and gives a *khutbah* but does not fulfill the other rules for *jumu'a*, then the entire thing is invalid. It is unfair and deceptive to those who follow.

The other reason I mention this is because of the unusual circumstances in which we live. Here in California, we are under orders to stay at home and to avoid public gatherings.[87] This means The Usuli Institute cannot hold its regular *jumu'a* in which around twenty people attend. We changed the location to have the minimum number required for a valid *jumu'a*. We have restricted it to people with whom we are already very close. As I have repeatedly emphasized, the very purpose of *jumu'a* is for a community to reflect upon its affairs and to remember the role that God plays in those affairs.

Religious services have been suspended all over the world to avoid contagion. This is because of orders to stay at home and because religious services are not considered essential services. It is interesting that legal services have been considered essential, meaning

---

87 Since January 2021, The Usuli Institute has relocated to Columbus, Ohio.

lawyers can continue to go to their offices to meet clients. Food markets are, of course, considered essential. The point to reflect upon is that what is considered essential is socially constructed and socially conceived. That physical therapy is considered essential but religious services are not, for example, is a social construct, and that social construct comes from one's values. As a Muslim, God is central to everything. There is no mental or physical health without God. In fact, the trial of this pandemic reminds us of the fool's errand of trying to create well-being without making God central to our existence. It is a social construct to imagine that physical health, mental health, and legal services are necessary, but religious services are optional. I am not suggesting that we should use religious services for people to freely mingle and infect each other. Yet one way of questioning the role of God in our lives is to recognize the role of religious services and to ask ourselves if these services are essential. If we consider religious services necessary, then we must be creative about finding ways to maintain these services while avoiding infection. If we had true scholars who knew the Islamic tradition, for example, we would know that there are many precedents in Islamic history when *jumuʻa* was held with a limited number of people who, instead of standing side-by-side, stood apart to avoid contagion during a plague. In our time, of course, they would have opened the windows, kept the doors open, and stood separated. In our modern age, we could at least have a valid *jumuʻa* and allow a limited number, say five or twenty, to stand apart. Then, on the basis of this valid *jumuʻa,* we could broadcast it for others to follow from home. The role of the *khutbah* here is critical. If there is a religious service but the *khutbah* is irrelevant, not saying anything to those experiencing social and economic trauma, then the service fails.

It worries and disturbs me when we withdraw the role of God, especially in the Muslim community. In the Jewish and Christian community, synagogues and churches have become very active during the pandemic. In the Muslim community, our mosques and Islamic centers have simply shut down. Instead of finding creative ways to hold the hands of the community, to bring a sense of comfort and peace, and to provide some form of counseling, assurance, and tranquility, our mosques are closed. This could involve helping those at risk of becoming homeless, collecting donations for those facing financial hardship, or supporting families at risk of losing their jobs. If you care about the Muslim *Ummah*, this is the correct ethic. Instead of becoming an active part of the solution in a pandemic, however, our mosques and Islamic centers have withdrawn to the margins.

Let me be clear. As a minority, we owe an obligation to civic society at large. We owe an obligation to the nation. We owe an obligation to the world. As a religious service, however, we first and foremost owe an obligation to our Muslim *Ummah* in the same way that a synagogue owes its obligation to its Jewish congregation and a church owes its obligation to its Christian congregation. If a Muslim community does not find its Islamic center holding its hands in this crisis, collecting donations, and organizing services to provide care and comfort, then that Islamic center has failed.

There is a core concept here. It is the concept of an *Ummah* premised on brotherhood and sisterhood. The first act of the Prophet in Medina was to declare the bonds of brotherhood between the *Muhajirun* and *Ansar*. This close brotherhood meant that these individuals fought each other's battles and cared for each other during financial hardship, illness, and even after death. The secret to the success of the early Muslim community was this bond of fidelity that made people feel a sense of pride, belonging, and loyalty. In

Arabic, it is sometimes called *'asabiyya* (social solidarity). It is the same pulse that animates nationalism, patriotism, and any other sense of belonging and fidelity. It is critical for a Muslim to actually *feel* like a Muslim. If a Muslim in a time of crisis cannot turn to his or her *Ummah*—and by "*Ummah*" I mean their local mosque—for real comfort and care, then we are lost. Real comfort is not just saying, "May God bless you, brother." It is to make an active effort to create a network so that if you lose your job, you will not become homeless. If a member of your family becomes ill, this network will meet the needs of the family. The role of the Muslim community is critical.

It distresses me when I see the response of Islamic centers is not to speak to or address the needs of the congregation, but to speak to the state. This is exactly what happens "back home" in the Muslim world. It is the same type of diseased mentality that plagues those who grew up under authoritarianism and despotism. They effectively tell the state: "Look, we are good boys and girls. We are following the instructions," and think they have done their job. So long as the state, the police commissioner, and the mayor are happy with them, they think that they have performed their role.

I bring this up because Muslims all over the world, particularly the younger generations, have lost any sense of confidence, loyalty, and fidelity to the concept of *Ummah*. God told us we are a single *Ummah* (Q 21:92) and yet most of the younger generations do not even care about the concept. They do not buy it. They say, "What *Ummah*? Muslims do not care about each other. I cannot count on Muslims for any type of comfort, peace, or support." This is a disaster. It is also key to our failures. Stop impressing those in power and pay attention to the substance of justice itself, for *that* is what brings God's blessings. God does not bless those who perform before power to impress power. God blesses true justice, mercy, and kindness. I know that during this crisis, many Muslims, particularly Chinese and Asian Muslims, have been subject to acts of racism because of the coronavirus. These Muslims should be able to turn to their community. One organization created a website that monitors acts of racism against Asians and reported its findings to authorities in the United States and the United Nations. It bothered me enormously that those behind this initiative were Christians. It should have been Muslims. All this is tied to an important point about the pandemic.

In the last *khutbah*, I reminded you and reminded myself that God sends hardship so that "perhaps you will turn to God" (Q 6:42).[88] This pandemic comes with so many lessons. I was reading several articles about how much money rich people have lost due to the pandemic. I said to myself, "If even ten percent of this money had been voluntarily donated to helping the impoverished, the undeveloped, refugees, or those displaced by war, genocide, racism, or religious bigotry, and if leaders, instead of being forced to lose this money through a pandemic, had voluntarily committed this money for worthy causes, would God have allowed the pandemic to hit the world the way it has?" The virus comes as a stark reminder of the immorality of the world we live in. Wealth is unequally distributed. The wealthy do not care about the suffering of the poor. I cannot ignore the fact that no one seems to know or count the number of infections and deaths among displaced refugees. No one knows the extent to which the virus has spread among Syrian refugees, the Rohingyas, or the Muslims in Chinese concentration camps. We simply do not know how many have died. But we know meticulously, down to the person, the number of deaths in Italy, Spain, and Germany. If you are from the White part of the world,

---

88 See Chapter 20: *Trials of a Prophet Loved and the Mirror of the Coronavirus* in this volume.

your life is valued on a different scale to those from the dark part of the world. Tell me: if you were the Maker of this universe and you saw this level of immorality, what would you do?

During these trying times, I want to remind especially young Muslims: God created you and God loves you. Were you to ask, "What is the evidence that God loves me?" Think for an instant. Reflect. You may not realize that consciousness and life itself is a gift, but it is. You may not realize how the power of reasoning and free choice is a gift, but it is. Every second of every day, look at how many things God blesses us with. Every time we use our eyes, find the words to express ourselves, talk to our friends, fill our stomachs, or see our loved ones safe, healthy, and smiling at us, it is all evidence of God's love. For God could have taken it all away. "And if you attempt to count God's blessings, you cannot, in fact, count them" (Q 16:18). We enjoy God's love all the time, but we take it for granted. When we ignore or are impatient with our loved ones, we take God's love for granted. When we hurt the feelings of our loved ones, neighbors, and society, we take God's love for granted. When we stop caring for the poor and needy and live selfishly and egotistically, we take God's love for granted. God does not create and hate. God creates and loves. God's love continues to bless and surround us despite our ingratitude, obstinance, and the fact that so many of us just slap it back, and say, "I do not notice it. I do not see it. I am busy. I have things to do."

Now we have a virus that has reminded the powerful that perhaps they are not so powerful. It has reminded us that but for the grace of God, a little virus can completely disrupt our lives. For some of us—may God protect us all—this virus can take our health, well-being, and everything we take for granted. It can even take our life. The only question is this: are we going to turn to God? Will we acknowledge God's blessings, and say, "I get the message. I hear You. I do not need to go through this trauma to acknowledge the fact that Your care, mercy, and love surrounds and embraces me every second of every day"?

Ultimately, we will reach the point of death. At that moment, we will either confront a terrifying reality, meaning angels that look like demons will notify us that the journey is over, or we will be received by angels who receive us and say, "*Salaam*," meaning tranquility and peace (Q 56:26). From the moment of my mother's death until we buried her, she had a smile on her face. I knew exactly where that smile came from. The angels had arrived to say, "*Salaam.*" That moment is coming for us all. Either the angels of terror or the angels of comfort and tranquility will meet us. Our fate depends upon what we have done with God's love. It is as simple as that. We can be idiots as much as we want. The Qur'an says most people will, in fact, live and die as idiots for they refuse the extended Hand that is filled with love and mercy (Q 2:243; 10:60; 25:60; 40:61). When we find ourselves infected with a virus in a critical condition in the hospital, however, all that nonsense evaporates. Suddenly, all our pretense, ego, and arrogance disappear as we mutter, "God, please save me."

I will close with a story. I knew a woman who used to be a practicing Muslim who wore *hijab*. She used to post "Proud to be Muslim" images on social media. This was until she became friends with some people in college. These friends took her down a wrong path. Within two years, not only had she left Islam, but she would brag on social networks that she was an ex-Muslim. She mocked religious people. Suddenly, this girl became gravely ill. She told her mother seconds before her death, "I am scared of what God is going to do with me. Please pray that God forgives me." She then died. This is a true story. After she died, of course, her mother and father had the question of whether to bury her as a Muslim. That is how I became involved with the case. Unfortunately, according to her father, she did not re-utter the *Shahadah* (testimony of faith). Her mother disagreed. There was conflicting testimony, but this is not the point. I share this story because this girl used to pontificate all her skepticism on social media. Yet when it comes to the moment of terror when you feel the shadow of death approaching, that is when you see the truth. That is when the truth is clear and crisp.

Do not be among the foolish. Know that God loves you and it is only your doubts and failures to reciprocate that love that make you unable to see this loving God, a God who gives, gives, gives, and continues giving.

20 March 2020

22

More on Virtual *Khutbah*s and the Personal Nature of a Pandemic

We must address once again the practice of virtual *jumu'a*. Recently, a representative of the International Association of Muslim Scholars (IAMS) appeared on *Al-Jazeera* and issued what amounted to a *fatwa* that effectively stated that virtual *jumu'a*s are *haram* and inconsistent with the laws of the *Shari'a*. There are several things to note here. The statement was made soon after the coronavirus crisis emerged and people all over the world were ordered to stay at home. I have noticed since the start of the pandemic that several virtual *jumu'a*s have popped up in different places because mosques have been shut down. Several groups have initiated what amounts to a virtual *jumu'a*. From what I have seen, however, they do not seem to have thought too deeply about what they mean by virtual *jumu'a*. In many cases, it entails no more than someone getting onto a podium in front of a camera, and saying, "I am giving a *khutbah*." They then say, "Now I am going to pray two *rak'ah*s for *jumu'a*. Follow me electronically." They are not even sure if anyone is praying behind them. This is seriously problematic. In my view, this type of *jumu'a* is null and void. As I have said previously, we cannot ignore the rules for *jumu'a*. We cannot simply have an *imam* who prays and does not know whether a quorum exists for *jumu'a*. That is not the idea of *jumu'a*.

I therefore understand the IAMS. Their point is that *jumu'a* was mandated in part so that Muslims can come together, meet face-to-face, shake hands, hug, converse, and offer *dhikr* before returning to their homes. In other words, so that a community of believers can physically come together and collectively worship God while representing a single nation, an *Ummah*. I understand the fear that if virtual *jumu'as* spread and become the norm, it will defeat the very purpose of *jumu'a* itself. From their perspective, then, even if there is a plague and we have to close mosques and suspend *jumu'as* for a time, there is simply no reason to create a *bid'a* in worship. Innovations in the realm of worship are a serious matter and require a compelling reason because ritual acts of worship have been decreed directly by God. We do not always know the reason for the ritual acts we perform, other than that God decreed it so. So we must exercise caution. This, then, is the logic of the IAMS. Even if there is an emergency, so what? There have been various epidemics in the past, especially in the Middle East, such as wars and plagues. *Jumu'a* was suspended until circumstances changed and people returned to the mosque, with no harm done. In fact, the representative of the IAMS said, "If you must, then have a lecture but pray the *Zuhr* prayer, not *jumu'a*. In that way we do not change the rules for *jumu'a*."

We have to take our *Shari'a* seriously. If we are irrationally restrictive and conservative, it does a lot of harm. But if we haphazardly do whatever we please regarding issues of worship, this will also unravel the *Shariʿa* and render it meaningless. But there are two additional factors to consider here.

First, I may agree with the IAMS as far as *jumuʿa* in Muslim countries is concerned. There are points to agree with, others to disagree with, but, ultimately, if *jumuʿa* is suspended for a period in these countries, once the crisis is over, mosques will reopen and *jumuʿa* will return. Mosques will once again be busy. No harm will be done. But we have a very different set of considerations for Muslims in non-Muslim countries. In non-Muslim countries, *jumuʿa* is often the only link that keeps Muslims connected to their tradition. *Jumuʿa* is often the only thing that makes Muslims feel part of an *Ummah*. There are so many challenges, distractions, and threats that can lead to the loss of a sense of Muslim identity. To be very blunt: especially for our younger generations, there is often nothing that makes them feel Muslim save for this one weekly event. This is unlike churches, which often have a host of activities associated with their worship. It is unlike synagogues, which have a host of practices that reaffirm a sense of pride in being Jewish. For Muslims, *jumuʿa*, for all practical purposes, is all there is—and it is very minimal. For many Muslims, *jumuʿa* lasts fifteen or twenty minutes. They pray, and they are gone. That is their Islam. For many others, even if they perform their daily prayers, daily life does not affirm any social bonds as a Muslim except for this one weekly event. So, there is a different set of priorities and needs for Muslims in the West. *Jumuʿa* is a lifeline for so many, particularly the youth. It is the one thing that reminds them that they are Muslim and belong to an *Ummah*. If that connection is severed for a period of time, we cannot casually say, "What is the problem? We will restore *jumuʿa* afterward." The sense of belonging of so many Muslims to an *Ummah* is so tenuous that it may not return. Many people, once mosques have reopened, may never come back.

This brings me to the second factor. If *jumu'a* plays this critical role among Muslims in non-Muslim countries, how can we respect the rules of the tradition that require a physical attendance, on the one hand, while serving the exigent circumstances that arise among Muslims, on the other? Here, the critical factor for *jumu'a* is that there is a sense of a collectivity coming together to worship God. Consider a group of people who intend to pray *jumu'a* virtually, not physically, because of the present circumstances. The rules for *jumu'a* are otherwise met[89] and the *imam* has agreed that the group will gather online under these exceptional circumstances. In my opinion, the rules on physical attendance have here been achieved electronically because these people have made the effort to come together to worship God. Put differently, I ask myself, "If the Companions lived in our age and confronted similar circumstances, what would they have done?" Particularly if they were in a place where Muslims had such a tenuous connection to their Islamic identity and community. Would they simply let the threats and challenges impact the community? Or would they use modern technology to creatively and daringly fulfill the official rules for *jumu'a*, while at the same time finding a compromise that achieves the purposes of the *Shari'a*? This is the important point.

I do not think the IAMS is correct as far as Muslims in the West are concerned. We have very different concerns and worries. We do not use the coronavirus as an excuse to let an essential act of worship and the blessings that come with *jumu'a* pass us by. If one is going to hold a virtual *jumu'a*, however, then please respect the rules. If it

---

89 This refers to the minimum requirement of the physical presence of four people for a valid *khutbah*. See Chapter 1: *The Usuli Institute's First Virtual* Khutbah in this volume.

cannot be done through physical attendance, let it be done through a meeting of the minds. Use modern technology to enable people to intentionally come together to offer *jumu'a* prayers.

This is connected to another important point. We are going through a real test and hardship. Some of our brothers and sisters have lost their jobs. Many of us have family members who are sick. The truth is that some of us have family members who will die. We ourselves may get sick and die. This is, of course, a source of stress, and part of belonging to a Muslim community is that we feel each other's pain. We do not deny it. We do not pretend it does not exist. We feel it and we respond to it. God reminds us that God has always sent trials and hardships to former people (Q 2:155; 6:42). The key challenge is this: where do you turn when hardship befalls you? Remember that the Prophet himself was confronted not only with the death of his wife, Khadijah, but also the death of his children, sons and daughters. Every son or daughter of the Prophet died in his lifetime, except Fatima. Even after the Prophet was victorious at Badr, the first battle and victory for Islam, he returned to Medina where the news awaited him that his daughter, Ruqayya, had died. She did not die from an accident, but from an infection. We have many reports of people in Medina dying suddenly, like Ruqayya. So many died young and inexplicably in medieval times. It was because of the circumstances of the age. Plagues were not only common, but seasonal. We can imagine that if this happened to us, with our modern minds, we would immediately think God had forsaken us, cursed us, and did not love us. We would immediately ask, "Why has God taken my child? I just fought a battle for God and was victorious for God's favor. Is this how God rewards me?" Hardships test our mettle. As the Qur'an so eloquently puts it, "We seized them with misfortune and hardship, that they might humble themselves" (SQ 6:42). Every challenge or loss is an opportunity to turn to God, recognizing our dependence on God and strengthening our relationship with God.

Under these trying circumstances, then, what do we do? First, assume that this affliction has come to talk to you directly. Do not use logic to marginalize and generalize the events and avoid self-reflection. Do not say, "This afflicts everyone. I will simply follow the rules and get on with my life. It is nothing personal." Rather, personalize it. For believers, every event that unfolds should be highly personal. How does that event speak to you and your relationship with God? Remember that God knows us as collectivities, as nations and tribes, but also as individuals.

Second, assume the worst. Pray and supplicate for the best but assume the worst. Assume that whatever you fear will happen. If you only worship God in times of hardship, you are a hypocrite. If you do not worship God until your child or parents are sick, for example, you are a hypocrite. Assume the worst. Assume that you will in fact get sick, be in critical care, and die. But commit to not being a hypocrite.

Third, remember that God instituted the laws of causation and that being a good Muslim means following these laws of causation. God makes no promise that the laws of nature will be suspended in your case because you are so special. The laws of causation are the laws of contagion, illness, and medicine. It is humble and pious to know the laws that apply to everyone else apply equally to you. Those who lack humility and take God for granted say, "It applies to everyone else, but not me." Are you somehow privy to a covenant with God (Q 2:80)? Are you the exception to the laws of causation? A Muslim does not think this way. A Muslim is a rational being who follows the laws of causation, recognizes their mastery, and does not assume the laws of causation will be suspended in their case. It is your Islamic obligation to follow all the rules of cleanliness and social distancing.

Lastly, do not tell yourself, "I have lived a life in which I never turned to God. I have failed myself so many times. I have committed so many sins. I have been a hypocrite with God so many times. Now that there is a serious threat, I am ashamed. I feel embarrassed to turn to God because I have been such a disappointment in the past." Remember that God says clearly that the real hypocrites are those who despair in God's mercy and forgiveness (Q 12:87; 15:56; 39:53).

This virus is an opportunity to come to God. Whether you ask God to keep you safe or not is your business. But nothing is worse than persisting in sin and not turning away from sin. Nothing is worse than willfully distancing yourself from your Maker because of what you have done in the past. If you are an oppressor, a tyrant, or a person who has committed many sins, this virus is a punishment for you and a warning. Perhaps you will get the point and return to God. If you have oppressed others, God is now oppressing and warning you. If, on the other hand, you have lived a just life and have not oppressed others, this virus is not a punishment but an opportunity to bring you even closer to God. You should welcome every such opportunity. Remember that the more you supplicate and beg God for closeness, the more your heart will feel tranquility and peace when you hear God's name (Q 13:28). So many people feel uncomfortable and nervous when the name of God is mentioned. This is because they have unresolved business with God. There are many unresolved things that embarrass them and make them feel uncomfortable before God. So, they escape from God. Ultimately, this is foolish. They will eventually die and face God. But human beings are foolish.

This virus is an opportunity for the unjust to remember their injustice and reform. It is an opportunity for the sinner to come back. And it is an opportunity for the most pious human being in the world to draw even closer to God. Think to yourself, "What if I, my child, or my loved ones get ill? How will my discourse with God be affected?" Commit to not becoming a hypocrite. Start now. Start your process of resolving the conflicts within and being at peace with your Lord. Do not wait until you receive the message in the most severe and drastic way. Always remember that God is the Most Merciful and the Most Forgiving. There is nothing God cannot forgive. And there is nothing that hides from God. If you think you have hidden something from the entire world, God has already seen it and already knows it. You are simply not being honest with yourself.

There are so many things from our majestic and wondrous intellectual and spiritual heritage that I want to share. Yet circumstances arise and *jumu'a* must address circumstances that are relevant to people. I want to underscore that so many Muslims will accept that *jumu'a* is the only thing that connects them to the Muslim *Ummah*. Yet they will say, "But we go to so many mosques and the *khutbah*s are terrible. They have nothing to do with anything. *Khutbah*s are occasions for people to show off their Arabic and cite the Qur'an or *hadith*s with no effort to exert their intellect or make the *khutbah* relevant." In many Muslim countries, *khutbah*s are carefully controlled by the government and overseen by the security forces. Such *khutbah*s are intentionally anachronistic, with no relevance to our day and age. Yet it *is* possible to challenge this dead discourse with some daring and honest speech. It *is* possible to demonstrate that colonialism failed to turn Islam into a dead religion. For *khutbah*s to challenge this authoritarian state of mind and awaken the dead spirit and intellect of the oppressed—for when you oppress a person, they die intellectually and spiritually; they no longer generate creativity because they first learn fear, and fear kills creativity—there must be *khatib*s who are committed to the principle of truth and who have a powerful conviction that unless they speak the truth, they will be punished rather than rewarded, because God does not accept untruthful or hypocritical speech.

To the Muslim *Ummah*, I say the following: perhaps there will be a cure for coronavirus, but there is no cure for stupidity. Sadly, there is nothing one can do to cure stupid people. Stupid people will read and understand things stupidly. There is no way to elevate their IQ. How, then, do we get people who are intelligent and educated, not stupid, onto the podiums of *jumu'a*? I am talking about here in the West. It is only you, the consumer, who decides. If stupid people speak from pulpits and find that Muslims still come to them, listen to them, and do not rebel against their stupidity, we will remain a colonized, dominated, and oppressed people. Only if Muslims rebel against this stupidity and insist that the space that represents God be respected and dignified will we start to see change. At present, no intelligent, educated, and accomplished person is drawn to the podium because they cannot build a rewarding career as a *khatib*. However, if the community starts to honor the space in which God is represented, then it may start to attract intelligent people. Perhaps intelligent people will then know that the Muslim community demands excellence and elevation in speech.

In the Muslim world, it is a different matter entirely. We have reached the point that one of the largest *fatwa* bodies in the Muslim world, *Dar al-Ifta' al-Misriyya*, has issued a *fatwa* against a Turkish drama show, *Ertrugrul*.[90] The true reason for this, regardless of what is claimed, is because Arabs who watch the show have come to admire Ottoman history and heritage, and the Egyptian government hates the Turks and the Ottomans. The official body for *fatwas* in Egypt has, therefore, taken an official position that it is *haram* to watch the show. The head of the Ministry for Religious Endowments in Egypt has said that the Muslim Brotherhood is behind the spread of the coronavirus. Look at the levels of absurdity that we have reached. The same ugly and evil factor is at play in all of them: despotism.

This is a powerful message to Muslims in the West who travel to Saudi Arabia, Egypt, or Mauritania, learn some Arabic, spew off Qur'anic verses, a *hadith* here and a *hadith* there, and then use this to attain a position of authority, but who, ultimately, do not elevate their intelligence. They import the demonic stain of despotism from Muslim countries to Muslims in the West. If you are a sincere Muslim, use that as a warning sign. They have traveled to corrupted places and imported to the West an Islam that is deeply infected with hypocrisy and despotism. From that, intelligence is stunted. The passion that animates religion is stunted.

It is time that we realize that our practices of *jumu'a* are full of stereotypical statements, buzzwords, and concepts that defy reason, logic, and beauty. It is time to rebel against them. It is time to make our religion more meaningful in our lives and in the lives of our children. Personally, when something like the coronavirus pandemic occurs, I do a lot of questioning. If I get sick and die tomorrow, have I done enough for my children to raise their heads as Muslims? Have I explained enough? What I most care about is the fate of my children. I reflect on this a lot. It is not the money,

---

90 For more on *Dar al-Ifta'*, see footnote 13.

job, career, or degrees. I most often think about how I want my children to grow up not only as Muslims, but as proud Muslims, and how, ultimately, I want to meet them in heaven. I ask myself these ultimate questions and I try to make my peace with God while I am still standing and still coherent. I advise you to do the same. Ask yourself: if you were to die tomorrow, what would most worry you? What would be the most important thing for you? If it is not that your child lives and dies as a proud Muslim, then something is wrong in your relationship with Islam.

27 March 2020

GLOSSARY OF TERMS

'Abbasids
The second ruling dynasty of the Muslim empire after the Umayyads. Flourished in Baghdad from 132/750 to 656/1258. Thereafter, it survived as a shadow Caliphate until 923/1517.

Adhan
A call to prayer recited five times a day before each of the communal prayers.

'Alawi
An esoteric offshoot of Shi'a Islam. Also known as Alawites or Nusayris.

Alhamdullilah
Often used expression that means "thank God," my gratitude be to God.

Allahu Akbar
The declaration, known as *takbir*, which means God is greater than all.

Ansar
The native inhabitants of Medina who believed in and supported the Prophet.

Asabiyya

Lit., the word implies a sense of "group feeling" or "social solidarity" with an emphasis on unity, shared purpose, and social cohesion. The idea is often associated with Ibn Khaldun (d. 808/1406) who saw *asabiyya* as a driving force of history.

'Awra

Areas of the human body that are considered private and to be covered in the presence of others. A modest man or woman would cover these parts of the body with loose-fitting cloth. Whether cultural norms may be considered in defining modesty is subject to debate. The parts that should be covered are different for men and women.

Azhar

Lit., the brilliant or the radiant. A mosque and university in Cairo established by the Fatimids in 358/969. The Azhar has graduated many religious scholars in the Muslim world.

Bid'a

Lit., innovation. Often refers to a heretical or illegal innovation in religion. *Bid'a hasana* means a good or desirable innovation. *Bid'a sayyi'a* is a bad or undesirable innovation.

Caliph

Arabic: *Khalifa* (pl. *khulafa'*) lit., successor or deputy. Refers to the head of the Islamic state after the death of the Prophet.

Companion

A term used to describe all those who converted to Islam and lived with the Prophet. Some Companions, however, such as Abu Bakr, 'Umar, and 'Ali, were particularly close to the Prophet or lived with him for a longer time.

Du'a'

A supplication or prayer.

Dhikr

Remembrance of God.

Fatwa

A non-binding legal opinion issued in response to a legal problem.

Fiqh

Lit., the word implies "an understanding." Islamic law: the process of jurisprudence by which the rules of Islamic law are derived. The word is also used to refer generally to positive law.

Fitra

The inner essence of an individual or the intuitive sense by which one recognizes right and wrong, the moral and the immoral.

Hadith

Lit., a report, account, or statement. Islamic law: a Prophetic tradition transmitted through a chain of narrators by which the Prophet or his *Sunna* is known. The word may also be used to refer to a statement by one of the Companions.

Hajj

The fifth pillar of Islam; pilgrimage to Mecca at least once in a person's lifetime, if physically and financially able to do so.

Halal

Islamic law: the permitted, allowed. Most schools hold that everything is permitted unless there is evidence requiring that it be prohibited. Most schools adhere to a presumption of permissibility, and so, the burden of proof is against the person who is arguing for a prohibition. *Halal* meat is meat slaughtered according to the specifications of Islamic law.

Hanafi

An adherent of the Sunni juristic school of thought named after its eponym Abu Hanifa (d. 150/767). The school developed in Kufa and Basra but spread in the Middle East and the Indian subcontinent. The Hanafi school is one of the four main Sunni jurisprudential schools.

Hanbali

An adherent of the Sunni juristic school of thought named after its eponym Ahmad Ibn Hanbal (d. 241/855). This school is one of four main Sunni jurisprudential schools of thought. Today, its adherents are found primarily in Saudi Arabia.

Haram

Islamic law: what is forbidden, the sinful, the prohibited. One of the five categories or values of *Shari'a,* connoting that which is forbidden or sinful.

Haram (pl. Haramayn)

Holy site. Used to refer to the "two holy sites" (*al-haramayn*) of Mecca and Medina.

Hasan

Lit., good, desirable. Islamic law: refers to that which is considered beautiful and moral as opposed to the ugly and immoral (*qabih*).

Hijab

Lit., obstruction, shield, shelter, protection, cover, screen, seclusion, obscure, and hide. The veil with which a Muslim woman covers her head, except her face. The face veil is call *niqab*.

Hijaz

A geographical region comprising most of the west of modern-day Saudi Arabia, including the two holy sites of Islam: Mecca and Medina.

Imam

Lit., one who stands out in front. Islamic law: leader of prayer or of a congregation. In common usage it often means a religious leader.

Imama

Lit. leadership. In common usage it often refers to the leadership of the Muslim community or congregation.

Ismaili

A sect of Shi'a Islam that broke from the main body of Shi'ism on the question of the line of *imam*s in succession to the Prophet, taking its name from the seventh *imam*, Isma'il b. Ja'far.

Jahiliyya or jahili

A state of ignorance, a state of misguidance. These terms are used to refer to the pre-Islamic period in Arabia. Often used to connote paganism or a state of darkness.

Jami

Jami Islam is closely related to Madkhali Islam, named after the writings of the Saudi Muhammad Aman al-Jami. See *Madkhali*.

Jihad

Lit., exertion, struggle. Jihad is struggle for the sake of God. The struggle could be one of self-discipline and self-purification or it could be an armed or unarmed struggle against oppression and injustice.

Jinn

A species of creation mentioned in the Qur'an. Reportedly, the *jinn* share certain attributes with human beings, such as free will, belief and disbelief, morality and immorality, procreation, and so forth. Satan was from this species of creation. Both humans and *jinn* differ from the angels insofar as the angels do not have free will to choose between right and wrong. Hence, Satan is not a "fallen angel" in Islamic theology.

Jumuʿa

Friday; the day of congregation in which Muslims gather at noon to hear a sermon (*khutbah*) in the mosque and offer the noon prayer. Unlike the Jewish or Christian Sabbath, Muslims are not required to refrain from work or rest on Friday or any other day. Although Muslims believe in six periods of creation, they do not believe that God needed to rest on the seventh period.

Kaʿba

Lit., cube. Refers to the house of worship built by Abraham and his older son, Ishmael, in the desert of Mecca. Muslims face the Kaʿba in their daily prayers as a symbol of their global unity.

Khalifa (pl. khulafaʾ)

Successors, deputies, or viceroys. According to the Qurʾan, human beings are the *khulafaʾ* of God on earth. Also see *Caliph*.

Khatib

Lit., a speaker. Usually, the term refers to the one who delivers the sermon (*khutbah*) before the noon prayer on Friday (*jumuʿa*).

Khutbah

Lit., a speech or lecture. Usually, the term refers to the sermon delivered on Friday (*jumuʿa*) before the noon prayer.

Kufr

Lit., to cover over something. In this sense, the term is found in the Qurʾan in its plural form as a reference to farmers (Q 57:20). Islamic law: covering over the truth once one has recognized it as true, i.e., rejecting the message of Islam. Also means ingratitude or infidelity, not believing in God or being ungrateful toward God.

Madkhali

Madkhali Islam is a subset of the broader Salafi-Wahhabi movement, named after the writings of Rabi' al-Madkhali. It is known for its emphasis on ritual orthopraxis, treating the details, mechanics, and technicalities of Islamic practice as the heart and core of the Divine will. Above all, Madkhalism is characterized by its rejection of democracy and modern human rights as blasphemies against the faith, its strict political quietism, and its doctrine of strict obedience to those in power—even if rulers are authoritarian, despotic, and unjust. Madkhali Islam holds that obeying those in power is a form of obeying the Divine will. For this reason, Arab governments such as the UAE have sought to promote Madkhali orientations at home and abroad. Madkhali ideas are not limited to Salafi-Wahhabis but have also become widespread among certain branches of Sufism.

Maghrib

Prayer performed after sunset. The fourth of the five daily prayers.

Mahdi

Lit., "the guided one." An eschatological messianic figure who, many Muslims believe, will appear at the end of the time to rid the world of injustice. Belief in the Mahdi is not an essential doctrine in Sunni tradition. In Shi'a tradition, the term refers to the twelfth and final *imam*, Muhammad al-Mahdi, who is said to be in a state of occultation (*ghayba*) from which he will eventually emerge.

Maliki

An adherent of the Sunni juristic school of thought named after its eponym Malik Ibn Anas (d. 179/795). One of the four main Sunni jurisprudential schools of thought. The school originated from the early jurisprudential schools of Medina. Today, it is widespread in North Africa and sub-Saharan Africa. This was also the school of thought that pre-dominated in Muslim Spain.

Mashallah

Lit., whatever God wills; Muslims utter the phrase to express awe, gratitude, or praise.

Miswak

Tooth-stick; a piece of stick with which the teeth are polished and cleaned, the end being made like a brush by chewing it so as to separate its fibers.

Mufti

Muslim legal scholar who is qualified to issue legal *responsa*. See *fatwa*.

Muhajirun

The migrants, Muslims from Mecca who believed in the Prophet and migrated with him to Medina.

Qarin

Lit., "a constant companion." A specific type of *jinn* that is unique to each individual. See *jinn*.

Rak'ah

A prescribed unit of the five daily prayers. A single unit consists of a ritual of bows, prostrations, and the recitation of prayers.

Rightly Guided Caliphs (al-khulafa' al-Rashidun)

In the Sunni branch of Islam these are the first four Caliphs: Abu Bakr, 'Umar, 'Uthman, and 'Ali. They are referred to as "the Rightly Guided" because they were esteemed Companions of the Prophet. Sunnis also believe that they were exceptionally just. Some Sunni scholars consider the Umayyad Caliph 'Umar Ibn 'Abd al-'Aziz to be the fifth Rightly Guided Caliph although he was not a Companion of the Prophet.

Ruku'

An act of bowing in prayer that precedes the full prostration. See *sujud*.

Salafi

The word *salaf* means "predecessors" and usually refers to the period of the Prophet and the Companions. The term invokes the authenticity and legitimacy of this archetypal generation. What it means to be a Salafi, however, is far from clear. The term, historically, has invoked a wide spectrum of quite contradictory thinkers and movements, each claiming to be an authentic representation or the beliefs and practices of the Prophet and Companions. Since the 1970s, the term has become increasingly associated, even interchangeable, with the Wahhabi school.

Shafiʿi

Adherents of the jurisprudential school of thought named after its eponym Muhammad Ibn Idris al-Shafiʿi (d. 204/820). This is one of the four main Sunni jurisprudential schools and is widespread in the Muslim world today.

Shahadah

Lit., derives from the verb *shahadah* which means to witness, see, or testify. Islamic theology: a testament of faith, to bear witness that there is but one God and that Muhammad is His Messenger. This is the first of five pillars of Islam (namely, the five are *shahadah*, *salah* (prayer), *sawm* (fasting), *zakah* (almsgiving) and *hajj* (pilgrimage).

Shariʿa

Lit., the water source, the way, the path. In Islamic theology and law, the path or way given by God to human beings, the path by which human beings search God's Will. Commonly misinterpreted as "Islamic law," *Shariʿa* carries a much broader meaning. It is the sum total of categorizations of all human actions. These categories are mandatory (*fard* or *wajib*), encouraged (*mustahabb*), permissible (*halal* or *mubah*), discouraged (*makruh*), and forbidden (*haram*). *Shariʿa* is not restricted to positive law per se but includes moral and ethical values, and includes the jurisprudential process itself.

Shaykh

Lit., old man, master, leader. The title is often used to describe a learned man or religious scholar.

Shi'a

Lit., party or faction; historically, a group among the Muslims that called for the rulership of 'Ali, the Prophet's cousin, after the Prophet's death. Today, the Shi'a are the second largest branch of Islam after the Sunnis.

Shirk

Polytheism or the association of partners with God. Believing in gods other than the One God.

Sira

Lit., this word derives from the verbal "*sara*" meaning, "to walk." Islamic theology: the biography of the Prophet (i.e., how he "walked" through life).

Sufi (Sufism)

Lit., one who wears a coat of wool. This term has been applied to Muslims who seek to achieve higher degrees of spiritual excellence or those who pursue Islamic mysticism or those who belong to a mystical order.

Sujud

Lit., prostration. The defining act of prayer in which a Muslim places his or her head on the floor while whispering supplications to God. Several *hadith*s of the Prophet indicate that God is closest to the believer when they are in this act of devotion.

Sunna

Lit., the way or course or conduct of life. Islamic law: the example of the Prophet embodied in his statements, actions, and those matters that he silently approved or disapproved as reported in *hadith* literature. The *Sunna* of the Companions means the precedent or the conduct of the Companions of the Prophet. *Sunna* is also the name used to describe the main branch of Islam.

Taghut

A word of Aramaic and Syriac origin connoting injustice, inequity, false deities, idolatry, oppression, tyranny, and despotism. *Taghut* is the very antithesis of the Qur'an's moral and ethical worldview.

Tawhid

Lit., unification, oneness. The Islamic doctrine of monotheism, *tawhid* connotes more than just numerical oneness. It is the idea that God is singularly unique, that all prayers and worship are due to God alone, and that God alone is the source of all that there is. The doctrine of *tawhid* rejects Christian Trinitarianism. Debates over the meaning and implications of professing *tawhid* underpin the diversity of Islamic thought. The various branches of the Islamic sciences, including philosophy, Sufism, and theology, all seek to explain the idea of God's oneness and unity.

Umayyads

First Islamic dynasty after the death of the Rightly Guided Caliphs. Established by Mu'awiya Ibn Sufyan after the death of 'Ali Ibn Abi Talib, and lasted from 41/661 to 132/750.

Ummah

The global community of Muslims.

Wahhabi

Follower of the strict puritanical teachings of Muhammad Ibn 'Abd al-Wahhab (d. 1206/1792). Wahhabis are hostile to the intercession of saints, visiting the tombs of saints, Sufism, Shi'ism, and rational methods of deducing laws. The Wahhabi creed is very restrictive of women. This creed dominates in Saudi Arabia.

Zaydi

One of three major branches of Shi'a Islam. Named after Zayd ibn 'Ali (d. 122/740), whom they followed as the *imam*.

Zuhr

Prayer offered at noon. It is the third of five prescribed daily prayers.

Selected Biographies

'Abduh, Muhammad (d. 1323/1905)

A famous Egyptian Islamic reformer of the thirteenth/nineteenth Century. He studied in Azhar. When exiled to Paris, he studied there as well and met Jamal al-Din al-Afghani (d. 1314/1897). 'Abduh emphasized that reform in society can only come gradually and must originate with changes in educational policies. 'Abduh emphasized the necessity of using reason in the development of Islamic law and emphasized the need for *ijtihad*. After the 'Urabi rebellion in 1300/1882, he was banished from Egypt but was allowed to return in 1889. Shortly after his return, he was appointed the Chief Mufti of Egypt and died holding that position.

'Aisha bint Abi Bakr (d. 58/678)

Abu Bakr's daughter and the Prophet's wife. 'Aisha played an important role in Medina during the Prophet's life. After the Prophet died, she became involved in politics and led a rebellion against 'Ali, the fourth Caliph. After her defeat in the Battle of the Camel, she retired to Medina where she continued to teach. She became a substantial juristic authority in her own right. She is the source of a large number of reports about the Prophet, and the source of many early legal opinions.

'Ali Ibn Abi Talib (d. 40/661)

Cousin, son-in-law, and a close Companion of the Prophet, 'Ali was one of the first converts to Islam in Mecca. 'Ali was, according to Sunnis, the fourth Rightly Guided Caliph (*rashidun*). During 'Ali's Caliphate, Mu'awiyah, the governor of Syria, rebelled against him, and this insurrection led to the Battle of Siffin in 657. After 'Ali was assassination by a member of the Khawarij rebels, Mu'awiyah declared himself Caliph. The supporters of 'Ali, *shi'at Ali* (the party of 'Ali), asserted the right of the 'Alid branch of the Prophet's family to the Caliphate, and led several rebellions against the Umayyads. This conflict eventually led to the sectarian division between Sunni and Shi'a. 'Ali was married to the Prophet's daughter, Fatima, and fathered the Prophet's two grandsons, Hassan and Husayn.

Abu Talib (d. 3 years before *hijra*/619)

Leader of the Banu Hashim clan and the Prophet's uncle, Abu Talib was a paternal figure for the Prophet, who was an orphan, and refused to cede to Meccan demands to silence or control the Prophet after he began openly preaching the message of Islam. The death of Abu Talib was a huge personal blow for the Prophet and led to an increase in Meccan persecution of the early Muslims, eventually culminating in the migration to Medina.

Alodah, Salman (b. 1376/1956)

An influential Saudi religious scholar and jurist with a mass following in the Arab world, Alodah is the author of numerous works, including a 2013 reflection on the Arab Spring, entitled *As'ilat al-Thawra* ("Questions Around the Revolution"), which argued that political despotism and tyranny were incompatible with Islamic theology. As of September 2017, Alodah has been in prison in Saudi Arabia for alleged "terrorism and conspiracy against the state."

Al-Afghani, Jamal al-Din (d. 1314/1897)

Teacher to Muhammad 'Abduh and considered one of the founding fathers of pan-Islamic unity and Islamic modernism. Much of al-Afghani's background, life, and career is shrouded in mystery. He was more concerned with promoting a united Islamic front against Western encroachments on the Muslim world than with the legal and theological differences among Muslims. Despite adopting the moniker "al-Afghani" (lit. "the Afghan") it is possible that he came from a Shi'a Iranian background and adopted the term "Afghani" to gain influence in Sunni circles.

Al-Kawakibi, 'Abd al-Rahman (d. 1319-20/1902)

A Syrian proponent of pan-Arab unity against the Ottoman Empire and a leading figure of early twentieth-century Salafism, sometimes called "enlightened Salafism," that embraced reason and the findings of modern science and condemned the alleged stagnancy of Muslim thought and the spread of 'superstition' in Muslim societies as an explanation for Muslim decline vis-à-vis the West. Al-Kawakibi wrote an influential condemnation of tyranny, widely seen to be against the Ottoman Caliph, entitled *Taba'i al-Istibdad wa-l-Masari' al-Isti'bad* ("The Nature of Despotism and the Demise of Enslavement").

Al-Khashoggi, Jamal (d. 1440/2018)

A Saudi dissident journalist, author, and columnist for *The Washington Post* who was assassinated inside the Saudi consulate in Istanbul in October 2018. The Saudi government initially denied reports of Khashoggi's death inside the consulate but later admitted that the murder was premeditated. By November 2018, the U.S. Central Intelligence Agency (CIA) had concluded that the assassination had been personally ordered by the Saudi Crown Prince, Muhammad Bin Salman.

Al-Qaradawi, Yusuf (b. 1345/1926)

An Egyptian Islamic scholar and jurist based in Qatar, chairman of the International Union of Muslim Scholars, and widely known as a "global mufti" on account of his worldwide influence and reach. Qaradawi is perhaps best known for his television program on the Arabic *Al-Jazeera* network, entitled *al-Shariʻa wa-l-Hayah* ("Shariʻa and Life"), which regularly attracted audiences in the millions.

Fatima al-Zahra' bint Muhammad Ibn ʻAbdullah (d. 10/632)

Daughter of the Prophet and Khadijah born in Mecca. She was eighteen years old when she married the Prophet's cousin, ʻAli Ibn Abi Talib, and migrated to Medina. She had four children with ʻAli: Hasan, Husayn, Umm Kulthum, and Zaynab. Her date of death cannot be established with certainty, but it is reported that she died within six months after her father's death. She was the only one of the Prophet's children to survive him. Fatima played a very important role in the life of the Muslim community in Medina and was a woman of exceptional piety and purity.

Hafiz (d. 793/1390

Khawje Sham al-Din Muhammad Hafiz Shirazi, more popularly known as "Hafiz" ("the memorizer"), was a Persian Sufi poet whose works are widely seen as the pinnacle of Persian literature. Best known for his collection of poems, called the *Divan*, which contains poetry that has since been memorized and used as everyday proverbs, up to the present day. A key feature of Hafiz's poetry is that of the ecstasy of Divine love and the theme of exposing hypocrisy, the latter of which is widely seen as a critique of the religious and political establishment of his time.

Ibn 'Arabi, Muhyiddin (d. 638/1240)

An Andalusian mystic, scholar, poet, philosopher, and saint who is widely known as *al-Shaykh al-Akbar* ("the Greatest Shaykh") and from whom the influential Akbari Sufi tradition takes its name. His cosmological teachings, including the influential doctrine of *wahdat al-wujud* (unity of being), have had a profound influence throughout the history of Islamic philosophy and spirituality, even though he did not use this term in any of his works. His major work is *al-Futuhat al-Makiyya* ("The Meccan Revelations") in which his mystical vision, theology, and metaphysics finds its most detailed expression. Critics of Ibn 'Arabi have accused him of blurring the essential line between God and God's creation. See *Ibn Taymiyya*.

Ibn al-Mubarak, 'Abdullah (d. 181/797)

An early Muslim scholar known primarily for his knowledge of *hadiths*. He is also the author of a famous book, known as a *musnad*, that contains reports about the Prophet and the Companions.

Ibn Qayyim al-Jawziyya, Shams al-Din Abu Bakr Muhammad Ibn Abi Bakr al-Zar'i (d. 751/1350)

A highly respected Hanbali jurist and theologian in Damascus, where he was born and where he died. He was the most famous pupil of the renowned scholar and jurist, Ibn Taymiyya. Ibn al-Qayyim's works on law were inspired and influential. He was also influenced by Sufism. He wrote several works in which he criticized several intellectual orientations, including the Ash'ari school of thought. For political reasons, Ibn al-Qayyim was imprisoned with his teacher Ibn Taymiyya in Damascus. He was not released until Ibn Taymiyya's death in prison.

Ibn Taymiyya, Taqi al-Din Ahmad Ibn 'Abd al-Halim (d. 728/1328)

A famous Hanbali jurist and theologian. Despite his Hanbali training, Ibn Taymiyya's knowledge was so great as to render him an independent *mujtahid*. At an early age, he migrated with his father to Damascus to escape the onslaught of the Mongol invasions. While there, his father was the director of the Sukkariyya School, where Ibn Taymiyya would receive much of his education and where he was later appointed as a teacher. Because of his polemics against his opponents and his political opinions, he was expelled from Damascus. He traveled to Egypt where he was imprisoned in Cairo and Alexandria. Eventually, he was allowed to return to Damascus, but his continued attacks against what he considered to be religious innovations and against Sufism, as well as his refusal to cooperate with the government, landed him in prison again, where he eventually died. It is reported that the entire city of Damascus went to Ibn Taymiyya's funeral. In addition to his own prolific writings, much of his thought and ideas are preserved in the writings of his most famous student, Ibn Qayyim al-Jawziyya. Ibn Taymiyya's exposition on theology named *al-Wasitiyya* and *al-ʿAqida al-Hamawiyya* was challenged as being heterodox. In the contemporary age, he has become a favored author among the Wahhabi movement, probably because of his criticisms against Sufism. His jurisprudence, however, is inconsistent with Wahhabi tenets.

ʿImara, Muhammad (d. 1441/2020)

An Islamic thinker, author, and editor who wrote well over one hundred works in the fields of Qurʾanic studies, Islamic history, theology and philosophy, and modern Muslim reform. He edited and published the works of Muhammad ʿAbduh, Jamal al-Din al-Afghani, and ʿAbd al-Rahman al-Kawakibi.

Khadijah bint Khuwaylid (d. 3 years before *hijra*/619)

She was the first wife of the Prophet and the first convert to Islam. A wealthy woman, she hired the Prophet before his calling and then proposed to him in marriage. She spent all her wealth supporting the persecuted Muslims in Mecca and died before the migration to Medina. The Prophet loved her dearly and was married to her for more than twenty-five years before she died.

Qutb, Sayyid (d. 1386/1966)

A major Islamic theorist and leading figure of the Muslim Brotherhood throughout the 1950s and '60s who was executed by the Egyptian government in 1966. Qutb wrote numerous works, including a popular and influential commentary of the Qur'an that was written during his time in prison. Aspects of his later thought, such as the necessity of overthrowing secular regimes, have been influential for radical groups, including Al-Qaeda.

Rumi, Jalal al-Din Muhammad (d. 672/1273)

A famous Hanafi jurist, Islamic theologian, and Sufi poet whose works have had an enormous impact on the history of Islamic spirituality. Rumi's works were written mostly in Persian. His famous *Masnawi* is arguably the most significant text in the history of Sufism, often called the "Qur'an in Persian," and widely seen as one of the greatest mystical works in world literature. After the Qur'an itself, it has been argued that the *Masnawi* is the most widely read text in Islamic history. Today, Rumi's works have been translated into many languages and he is often cited as the best-selling poet in the contemporary U.S. Many of these popular translations, however, should be read with caution; one finds a notable tendency to downplay the Islamic character of Rumi's poetry, including the many explicit and implicit references to the Qur'an and the Prophet Muhammad.

Ruqayya bint Muhammad (d. 2/624)

A daughter of the Prophet from his wife Khadijah. She married 'Uthman Ibn 'Affan, the Companion of the Prophet, who was later appointed as the third Right Guided Caliph after the death of 'Umar Ibn al-Khattab. She died during the Prophet's lifetime.

FURTHER READING

Works by Khaled Abou El Fadl

And God Knows the Soldiers: The Authoritative and Authoritarian in Islamic Discourses (Lanham, MD: University Press of America, 2001) analyzes the case study of a *fatwa* that supported a Muslim basketball player's refusal to stand up for the American national anthem. The book documents the rise of authoritarian, as opposed to authoritative, methodologies in modern Islam. The book is a revised and expanded edition of an earlier work; see *The Authoritative and Authoritarian in Islamic Discourses: A Contemporary Case Study*, 3rd edition (Al-Saadawi Publications, 2002).

Speaking in God's Name: Islamic Law, Authority, and Women (Oxford: Oneworld, 2001) analyzes the interplay between author, text, and reader in the construction of meaning. With a particular focus on Islamic law and women, the book explores the demise of the juristic tradition and the rise of authoritarian discourses in modern Islam by examining a range of *fatwa*s by leading Wahhabi clerics.

Rebellion and Violence in Islamic Law (Cambridge: Cambridge University Press, 2001) is the first systematic study of the idea of political resistance and rebellion in Islamic law. The book uncovers a highly technical and sophisticated discourse on the legality of rebellion, rebutting Orientalist notions that medieval Islamic political thought was characterized by political quietism and a doctrine of strict obedience to rulers.

The Great Theft: Wrestling Islam from the Extremists (New York: HarperOne, 2005) offers a primer on modern Muslim thought and exposes the hypocrisies, inconsistencies, and intolerance intrinsic to Wahhabi Islam.

The Search for Beauty in Islam: A Conference of the Books (Lanham, MD: Rowman & Littlefield, 2006) is a collection of essays inspired by the search for what is beautiful in Islam, about Islam, and among those who practice Islam. This search is often negotiated through an unflinching look at the ugly realities of modern Islam. A landmark publication that has since become a classic in the field.

Reasoning with God: Reclaiming Shari'ah in the Modern Age (Lanham, MD: Rowman & Littlefield, 2014) explores the true meaning of *Shari'a* and the way it can revitalize modern Islam. The book calls upon Muslims to re-engage the ethical tradition of their faith and explore the Qur'an's moral trajectory in the modern world.

Other works

Anne Norton, *On the Muslim Question* (Princeton: Princeton University Press, 2013) analyzes how since 9/11, Islam has become a scapegoat for Western fears and anxieties. The title of work evokes Karl Marx's famous 1843 essay, "On the Jewish Question," which discussed Jewish integration as a litmus test for Europe's commitment to Enlightenment values of liberty, equality, and fraternity.

Ben Hubbard, *MBS: The Rise to Power of Mohammad Bin Salman* (New York: Crown, 2021) offers a disturbing insight into the character of the current Crown Prince and future King of Saudi Arabia, Muhammad Bin Salman.

Darren Byler, *In the Camps: China's High-Tech Penal Colony* (New York: Columbia Global Reports, 2021) draws on private interviews with camp workers and detainees, ethnographic research in the region, and thousands of government documents to expose China's mass incarceration of Uyghur Muslims. The author is an expert on Uyghur society and Chinese state surveillance.

Michael Prior, *The Bible and Colonialism: A Moral Critique* (Sheffield, England: Sheffield Academic Press, 1997) explores how the Biblical narratives of the Exodus from Egypt and the conquest of Canaan, in addition to the Biblical claim of a Divine promised land, was co-opted to sanction the extermination of indigenous peoples by Western colonial powers. The book focuses on Palestine, South Africa, and Latin America.

Muhammad al-Ghazali, *The* Sunna *of the Prophet: The People of* Fiqh *Versus the People of* Hadith, ed. Abdalhaqq Bewley and Muhammad Isa Waley and trans. Aisha Bewley (London: Dar al-Taqwa, 2001) is an English translation of an iconic work by one of the greatest Muslim jurists in the contemporary age. The work is a searing critique of the ahistoricism, irrationalism, and intolerance of the Wahhabi school. The work became the author's most controversial work and was banned in several Muslim countries.

Thomas S. Kidd, *American Christians and Islam: Evangelical Culture and Muslims from the Colonial Period to the Age of Terrorism* (Princeton, NJ: Princeton University Press, 2009) explores how evangelical Christians have long seen Islam as both an "evil" religion and hostile threat to Christianity, while also seeking to convert Muslims to the Christian faith. The book shows how these historical trends were exacerbated by the events of 9/11 and the subsequent "War on Terror." It also exposes evangelical anxieties about the alleged Islamic "threat" from within the U.S. from groups like the Nation of Islam and America's immigrant Muslim population today.

Zareena Grewal, *Islam is a Foreign Country: American Muslims and the Global Crisis of Authority* (New York: New York University Press, 2014) explores what it means to be Muslim and American in the contemporary world, with a particular focus on notions of identity, belonging, uprootedness, and alienation among American Muslims.

INDEX

Halima, 197
Hanafis, 8–9, 230
Hanau shooting, 180–181
Hanbalis, 230
haram
    defined, 230
    determining validity of
        pronouncements about,
        92–94, 96
    virtual *jumu'as* as, 215
haram (holy site), 231
hardships, sent by God, 220–221
hasan, 231
hearing loss, author's, 170, 185
Higgs boson particle, 79
hijab, 20, 147, 212, 231
Hijaz, 52, 156, 231
honesty, with God, 163
human trafficking, 73–74
hypocrisy, 25
hypocrisy, according to Qur'an,
    167

I

Ibn al-Mubarak, 'Abdullah, 99,
    246
Ibn 'Arabi, Muhyiddin, 245
Ibn Qayyim al-Jawziyya, Shams
    al-Din Abu Bakr Muhammad
    Ibn Abi Bakr al-Zar'i, 71, 246
Ibn Taymiyya, Taqi al-Din Ahmad
    Ibn 'Abd al-Halim, 71, 246
Ibrahim, 196
Idlib, Syria; bombing of, 34
idols. *see taghut* (idols; injustice and
    inequity)
imama, 6, 231
imams. *see also* leaders, Muslim,
    evaluation of
    air of superiority of some, 64
    defined, 231

evaluating, 20–21
    sponsoring despotism, 169
'Imara, Muhammad, 193–194,
    247
India
    Assam massacre and, 189
    discrimination against
        Muslims in, 125, 130, 190
    genocide in, 131
    war against Kashmir, 189
information, power of, 110
innovation (*bid'a*), theological, 95
intellect, in Islam, 103–104
International Association of
    Muslim Scholars (ISMS),
    215–216
Iraq, suffering of Muslims in, 84
Islamic Center of Southern
    California, 10, 32–33, 191
Islamophobia, 101–102, 103, 109,
    111–114, 114, 116, 125, 126,
    180–181, 183, 188–189, 190,
    192, 198
Ismaili Islam
    defined, 232
    polytheistic tendencies in, 122
Israel
    criticism of as "anti-semitism,"
        125–126
    oppression of Palestinians and,
        130–131
Israelites, polytheism and,
    120–121

J

jahiliyya (a state of ignorance), 125,
    232
Jami Islam
    defined, 232
    deification of rulers and, 29,
        123

Y
Yemen, genocide in, 61, 65, 81, 84,
    97–98, 166, 171, 189
Yusuf, Hamza, 65, 127, 150–152

Z
Zaydi theology, 123, 240
Zaytuna College, 126–127, 181
Zuhr, 8, 84, 216, 240

ABOUT THE AUTHOR

*D*r. **Khaled Abou El Fadl** is the Omar and Azmeralda Alfi Distinguished Professor of Law at the UCLA School of Law, and founder of the Institute for Advanced Usuli Studies (The Usuli Institute). He is a classically trained Islamic jurist. He is the author of numerous books and articles on Islam and Islamic jurisprudence. Among his books are: *Reasoning with God: Reclaiming Shari'ah in the Modern Age, The Search for Beauty in Islam: A Conference of the Books, Speaking in God's Name: Islamic law, Authority and Women, And God Knows the Soldiers: The Authoritative and Authoritarian in Islamic Discourses, The Great Theft: Wrestling Islam from the Extremists,* and *Rebellion and Violence in Islamic Law.* He is the recipient of the American Academy of Religion (AAR) 2020 Martin E. Marty Award for the Public Understanding of Religion.

ABOUT THE EDITOR

*D*r. **Josef Linnhoff** holds a PhD in Islamic Studies from the University of Edinburgh, Scotland, U.K. His work has been published in *The Muslim World, Islam and Christian-Muslim Relations,* and *Critical Muslim.* He is Editor-in-Chief of *Project Illumine: The Light of the Quran,* a multi-year project at The Usuli Institute to publish the first English-language Qur'anic commentary in over forty years. Before joining The Usuli Institute, he worked as a Researcher for BBC Monitoring in London.

Made in the USA
Monee, IL
09 May 2022

41a33d0f-178a-4556-94d2-87b04b795deeR01